THE ART of the SLOW FLIP

By

Scott Jelinek

About the Author

Scott Jelinek has been a full-time real estate investor for nearly 30 years and has closed well over 800 deals. As of this printing, he owns 138 "slow flip" houses, with many more in the pipeline. His creative investment strategy, the "slow flip," involves buying houses with no money or credit and turning them into steady monthly income on a five-year timeline, without rehab, repairs, or the usual landlord headaches. He has taught many seminars and classes, showing people how to create long-term wealth through real estate investing. Now, he is on a mission to help as many people as possible set themselves free through real estate investing.

To my wife, Lisa

Who knows where I would have ended up without you.

Special thanks to all of my coaching clients and students,
who keep me motivated as they reach new levels of success.

Contents

Introduction

Slow Flips: The Fastest Way to Build True Wealth

I am well aware that the title of this book sounds like a contradiction. *Slow* flip? Isn't the whole point of "flipping" properties to do it quickly? In fact, isn't speed part of the definition? Yes, according to most sources.

The popular website, Investopedia defines "flipping" in real estate as "purchasing an asset with a short holding period with the intent of selling it for a quick profit rather than holding on for long-term appreciation." A Bankrate guide for beginning investors states that flipping occurs "when someone buys a property, holds onto it for a short time, and then sells it (the flip part) for a higher price."

So, what is a "slow" flip? My general definition is *the process of flipping a property as slowly as possible for the fastest path to wealth.*

Most readers know what we mean by "flipping." The general idea, as stated above, involves buying a house or other property for a low price and then selling it for a high one to make a profit. How can doing this *slowly* be the *fastest* path to wealth?

I'll answer that question in depth in the pages that follow, but to give you a quick preview, the seeming contradiction has everything to do with how we define "wealth." The slow flip is not the fastest possible path to a big check or a fat bank account (wholesaling houses, which I also do, is faster for quick cash), but I don't equate either of these things with "wealth."

A big check is spent, and then, you have to work hard to earn another. And another. A fat bank account dwindles over time and must be replenished again through hard work. By "wealth," I mean passive income, more money coming in than going out, without the need for work—unless you consider cashing checks work. A deep well that, through initial hard work, foresight, and a careful system, will replenish itself endlessly.

I've chased big checks and invested in real estate the conventional way, which prioritizes speed, debt, and leverage. It worked well until it didn't. I quickly built a fat bank account and an impressive empire, with more than 80 properties and close to a million dollars in cash, on hand. I drove fancy cars and had the best of everything, and I lost it all when the market crashed in 2008.

Never again, I told myself. I knew there had to be a better way—one that involved less risk, less debt, and more long-term financial stability. As I'll explain in Chapter 1, my system of slow flipping evolved from the pain of the Great Recession and my frustration that once the dust settled, the "experts" went back to teaching the exact same things that buried so many of us between 2007 and 2010.

What I'm presenting here is something very different from typical investing, not a get-rich-quick scheme, but a get-wealthy-gradually plan. There are many ways to make money in real estate. The method of slow flipping that I'll teach in this book involves less risk, less debt, and more peace of mind than most approaches. It does not involve using your own money, taking out big bank loans, or jeopardizing your credit.

It doesn't require hiring contractors, plunging toilets, or fielding midnight calls from disgruntled tenants.

Bankers don't do any of those things, and as we'll explore in detail, with slow flipping, you essentially act as a bank. You become the middleman, putting deals together, arranging the financing, and creating value for others, as well as long-term wealth for yourself.

Sounds too good to be true? It isn't. I've done hundreds of slow flips, and once you understand the process, it is relatively straightforward.

In the method of slow flipping I'll teach in the following chapters, we buy distressed houses cheaply, using private money. When you use private money, you don't need good credit or collateral (other than the houses you're purchasing). I'll show you how to find the kinds of ugly houses we prefer at the perfect price point. I'll also explain private money, which is plentiful once you understand how it works. It comes at a much higher interest rate than you could obtain from a bank precisely because there are no credit checks or other requirements. We don't mind the high-interest rate, though, because as you'll see, we're borrowing a comparatively small amount and paying it off quickly, within five years.

Why would someone loan you tens of thousands of dollars without credit, references, or a track record? It is because, in a typical scenario, you're borrowing $30,000 for a house worth $80,000. If you pay a private-money lender off, they get a great return, in the neighborhood of 12 percent. If you don't, they get a house worth $80,000 for $30,000, even better.

We then sell the house, as it is—no cleanup or rehabbing—with long-term owner financing. We put it on the market immediately at a hefty markup. The average price when I resell that $30,000 house is $89,000. A buyer purchases the house, typically with $3,000 to $5,000 down and a monthly payment of $875 over 30 years. That $875 payment covers your monthly payback of around $670 to the private-money lender, as well as taxes and insurance, for the next five years.

As I said, this is not a get-rich-quick scheme. With a slow flip, you break even for five years. After that, you own the house free and clear, and the monthly payment you're collecting goes into your bank account. If you're doing the math here, a monthly installment of $875 from your buyer adds up to $315,000 for 30 years. That is right; a payout of $315,000 on the house you bought for $30,000.

Why wouldn't the buyer find his own house for $30,000 rather than paying you all that dough? Because with your house, the buyer only needs $3,000 down and $875 a month, with no credit check. Many people who want to own don't have $30,000 or $40,000 to buy a distressed house in the neighborhood. They can't raise private money, or they've never even heard of it. They might also have shaky credit and limited funds, but they can swing that down payment and $875 a month, which makes your house attractive.

If one of these buyers goes the distance over 30 years, you make more than a quarter of a million dollars, but few, if any, will. Most will give you the house back, in which case, you sell it again, or they will sell it themselves. If that happens, you still win, getting $80,000 for a property you paid $30,000 for. You can then use that money to buy more houses and do more slow flips.

I've given a very quick overview of how slow flipping works here because I want you to understand upfront that this is a proven, concrete path to true wealth. It might seem confusing now, but I have dozens of students each year who begin with zero real estate knowledge and are slow flipping multiple properties successfully within a few months. We'll go over every step of the process, with concrete tips, pitfalls, contingencies, and complications. I'll show you how to find private money, look for properties, use a brag book, and develop an elevator pitch. We'll explore easy ways to harness Craigslist, Facebook Marketplace, signage, direct mail, and more to close deals.

When you finish this book, you will have your teeth firmly around the process and know everything you need to start slow flipping, feet firmly planted on the fastest possible path to wealth. What's more, is that you'll be armed with this knowledge as we enter an unprecedented wave of opportunity for slow flipping. As we'll explore later, the COVID pandemic and government-imposed moratorium on evictions created a deep pool of frustrated, angry landlords who want out of the business. Each one represents an opportunity for slow flips, in some cases, dozens of opportunities. To put this in context, after a lifetime of investing, I have 138 slow-flip properties as of this printing. A year from now, I expect that number to double, and in the pages that follow, I'll explain how you can tap into the coming surge in order to build wealth.

Earlier, I asserted that true wealth is about passive income—more money coming in than going out, with no work or stress on your part. That is the general idea, but how much money? How many slow flips do you personally need for true wealth? If you're happy with a modest home, a car, and the occasional dinner out, the number might be quite low. If your heart is set on a racing sailboat and European vacations, you'll need a lot more.

This is not a frivolous question. How much steady passive income do you require to be comfortable and happy? The answer is different for each reader, and in Chapter 1, I'll help you explore yours. The last thing you want to do is go all-out, making as much money as you possibly can for decades, and then hope there's a little time left at the end to enjoy it. Deciding upfront what's important to you and the kind of lifestyle you want will dictate how much money will be going out and how much you'll need coming in. It will help you decide on the number of slow flips you need to reach freedom and form a plan that puts you on the fastest possible path to wealth as you define it.

1

Build Your Vision, Your Wealth

Before we get into the nuts and bolts of slow flipping in Chapter 2, I want to help you explore what true wealth means to you. Most people reading this book think they just want to make money, but the title on the cover doesn't promise the fastest possible path to "money." People don't actually want money; they want what it can buy. The most important thing money buys for most people is freedom—freedom from worry, dead-end jobs, crushing bills, and the grunt work keeping us from our families and true passions. Real wealth means achieving that freedom, however, you define it. Money is simply the means to that end.

If you're tempted to roll your eyes right now and skip ahead to Chapter 2, please bear with me. Fifteen years ago, I would have skipped ahead too, and that failure to think about what I really wanted—the big-picture view of wealth—landed me in hot water. I wasted an enormous amount of time and resources thinking that if I just made as much money as I could as quickly as I could, everything would fall into place. It seemed to, for a while, and then, as I said, it emphatically didn't. My whole approach to slow flipping, the method I'll teach you here, started with rethinking what true wealth meant, what was important to me, and how I wanted to spend my days.

So, this isn't some crunchy therapy session or vague feel-good exercise. It is a vital first step in forming your personal business plan and the key to how you'll approach slow flipping.

First, let me back up to tell you a little about myself, how I came to focus on wealth rather than money, and how that new mindset led me to slow flipping as the fastest possible path to achieving my goals. I want you to understand why I think the way I do because many readers, I'm sure, are having similar experiences and looking for a better way.

How I Got Here

I grew up in New York, where I dropped out of high school in 11th grade. I always mention this when I do seminars because skeptics will inevitably say, "Sure, investing is easy for you, with your education and degree." Nope. I have no degree and a formal education that stopped at the 11th grade. I never went back to school, but that isn't the only place to learn. I pursued my own kind of education through seminars, books, self-development, and hard knocks—plenty of them.

Shortly after leaving the 11th grade, I joined the Army, at 17. Recruiters came to the mall where I worked and hit me up. I laughed and said, "I would love to, but I'm not 18 yet."

They said, "You can join at 17, with your parents' permission."

"Okay," I said, "Sign me up."

I stayed in the Army for a short time and then returned to Long Island with no special skills or training. Back in 1922, I moved to Virginia (here's where I start to feel old), and I got into a simple business— mowing lawns. I still tell people that if they don't have money and can't find a job, grab a lawn mower! Anyone willing to work can make $100 to $200 a day cutting grass.

I didn't have any interest in real estate back then and like most people, thought that I didn't have the kind of money, credit, or job you needed to buy property. In 1994, I was twenty-one and renting a townhouse with my sister for $675 a month when my brother brought me a flyer that forever changed my life. The page he found stuck to his front door advertised a townhouse for sale in his area. Anyone could buy this house for $5,000 down, according to the flyer. *No credit; no job? No problem!* It was a non-qualifying assumable mortgage. These arrangements disappeared later, but in the early '90s, non-qualifying assumptions allowed anyone to take over a mortgage, with no qualification necessary—a great opportunity for new investors.

"Why not?" I thought. Owning is better than renting, right? I made an appointment to see the house and tucked $5,000 in cash in my pocket. The agent gave me a tour. I pretended to understand what I was doing when in reality, everything I knew about real estate fit on that flyer.

After about five minutes of careful consideration, looking as worldly as I could, I pulled out my five grand. "I'll take it," I said, ready to exchange the money for keys.

"Hold on," she said, smiling. "We need to write a contract and have a closing."

This was my first lesson in real estate. The second lesson was that $5,000 down isn't actually $5,000. After closing costs, insurance, title policy, and other expenses, my total came to about $7,000. I scrounged up the additional money and closed on my first house. My mortgage payment was about the same as my $675 rent. Only now, I was an owner.

I kept mowing lawns, primarily around townhouses. I was charging $10 per lawn, but they were tiny, and I could walk from house to house, so it was efficient. About three weeks after I moved into my new house, a crude sign scrawled in Magic Marker popped up in the neighborhood: *House for $2,000 down, take over payments!*

I didn't know anything about real estate, but I could do basic math. I'd just bought a house with $5,000 down, and here was another non-qualifying assumption for just $2,000 down. I'd been ripped off!

In hindsight, I know that my reaction makes no sense. The amount down has no bearing on value, but in my head, this one was three grand cheaper, a better deal (It's ironic that the way I started buying then is a lot like the way I sell now, as we'll explore shortly).

I was annoyed about "overpaying" for my house, but then, a great idea struck. Why not buy the other house too? In my head, I averaged out the cost of the two houses to about $3,500 each, which would take the sting out of that first, larger down payment. I was starting to think like an investor, a completely naïve and inexperienced one, but still, I'd been bitten hard by the real estate bug. That second house triggered dreams of empire. I loved the idea that I could borrow money and tenants would pay it back.

I purchased the second house and found a tenant who paid $675 a month to rent it, about the same amount as my mortgage payment. Readers who have rentals know that this was not a good business plan. I was a child at the time, though, and didn't think much beyond the down payment and the idea that someone else would pay off my mortgage. What's not to like?

This was the birth of what I call my "McDonald's Plan." It didn't really have anything to do with McDonald's. I've never been employed under the golden arches. The idea was that if I bought a million dollars' worth of property (about 15 houses at the going rate, I figured), I could get a job at McDonald's, or anywhere, and simply wait. It wouldn't matter how big my checks were or where I worked. I'd be paying off those fifteen mortgages year after year, and in time, I'd be a millionaire.

Good plan, right? Sure, except that I didn't factor in some key things—vacancies, repairs, maintenance, and deadbeat tenants. I was charging about the same amount that I was collecting, with no buffer. It might not the smartest system, but it got me into real estate.

Soon, I was obsessed and buying up everything I could. Mowing lawns allowed for great recon, and I kept my eyes peeled for signs on my route, as well as on regular drives through the neighborhood. The other quaint method of finding deals back then, one some younger readers might not know, involved this thing called "the Saturday paper." In pre-Internet days, it was "the" place to find deals.

Every Saturday, I combed the newspaper for non-qualifying assumptions. Some required as little as $500 down; most needed $1,000 to $5,000. I kept picking them up, and by 2001, I had about 20 properties.

A Boom, a Bust, and a New Strategy

In 2001, as readers who were in real estate will remember, we had our first little taste of appreciation after more than a decade of stagnant prices. Most of my townhouses sold around the $65,000 mark back then (they are worth about $190,000 to $200,000 now). One day, I called on a house for sale, and the owner told me she wanted $90,000. Huh? I thought she was out of her mind. Three months later, she wanted $125,000.

Something was changing. By this time, I did know something about real estate, and I realized that values were climbing. I was going to all the seminars coming through town and reading the popular real estate books, and everybody taught the exact same thing, which is what they're still teaching: Pull the equity out of your properties and use that money to buy more properties. Take as much cash out as you can and buy as much as you can as quickly as you can. Leverage, leverage, leverage!

Well, I had some houses I owed about $60,000 each on. Suddenly, they were worth $125,000, then $150,000, so I did what everyone taught me to do. I pulled out the equity and used it for down payments on more houses. I was buying some conventionally, some "subject to" (an agreement with homeowners to take over their mortgage), and others as non-qualifying assumptions, like my first purchases.

My plan (well, "approach." "Plan" might be too strong a word) worked really well. In fact, I was crushing it. I worked my way up to a portfolio of 84 properties—nice big Virginia Beach houses, all heavily leveraged. But leverage was good, remember? Everyone taught what's called the "BRRRR" method of investing. That stands for "Buy, Rehab,

Rent, Refinance, and Repeat," the conventional way of flipping property. Without getting deep into the details, BRRRR insists that equity is dead money, a total waste if it's not earning you a return. Pull that equity out and put it to work for you. I did, and it did work for me, to the tune of more than 80 houses! I was a huge success in the world's eyes. "Scott, what does he have to worry about, with all that property?"

Well, one thing I wish young Scott had worried more about was the fact that 84 houses meant he had 84 mortgages and an enormous amount of risk. As long as the market was humming along, though, it was hard to see that risk. I never crossed into a million dollars, but I had just under $1 million in cash saved and 84 rental properties. I drove a Cadillac XLR convertible that cost $105,000, owned two Escalades, and lived in a nice house.

Then, in 2007, things shifted a little. Everybody talks about 2008, but I remember vividly that in 2007, we began to feel the first inklings of a downturn. Those slight signs of softening turned apocalyptic in '08, and overnight, 30 to 40 percent of my tenants stopped paying. They simply couldn't. Everybody talks about the "real estate crash," but it was an economic crash. Every industry and every sector of the economy was battered.

What could I do? When tenants stopped paying, of course, I had to make up the difference. Luckily, I had nearly $1 million in cash on hand, right? That sounds like a lot, but not with my mortgage liability. Apart from overhead and expenses, I had to send $20,000 to $30,000 a month in mortgage payments just to keep everything rolling, and I did until I ran out of money.

In hindsight, I obviously would have done things differently. At the time, though, we kept thinking, "This is it. This is the bottom. It can't get any worse." But it did get worse. And worse. And worse.

I fought the good fight until I ran out of money, and then, the mortgages on my houses fell behind. My whole business model was upended. I was the stop-foreclosure guy, helping people in danger of foreclosure unload houses before lenders took them. Now, my houses were being yanked by the bank. I lost about 55 homes to foreclosure. It got to the point where I sat down with a list of my properties, circling the ones I would fight to keep and letting nature run its course with the rest.

I managed to save some houses, which I'm grateful for, but it was a hard time. Most people got out of real estate then. They went back to their jobs at IBM or wherever, the lives they'd led before the boom. Not me. I always say that I was lucky not to have a fallback plan. If I couldn't do real estate, what else could I work at? The answers always came up short. I'd need a job as a brain surgeon just to maintain my life, and I was sure no one wanted me scrubbing for surgery.

Most of the investors I knew disappeared. I never saw them again, but some were flourishing, mostly older guys. Many of them were my lenders and continued to loan me money for rehabs. They were loaning everybody money, actually, not just doing well during the bust, but better than ever. How?

I didn't get it, but you can bet I paid close attention. I rekindled friendships with some of these older investors and treated the relationships differently, eager to pick their brains. What did they know that the rest of us didn't? They never realized that our lunches were actually interviews, but over sandwiches and bottomless coffee, I fired a steady barrage of questions, determined to learn their secrets.

The one thing that held true for all the investors who proved impervious to the bust was that they owned all of their properties, 100 percent, free and clear. Every! Last! One! They collected money, loaned money, and owned their assets, with no debt. If you'd asked me about this scenario in 2004, '05, or '06, I'd have called them idiots. Debt, according to all the gurus, was the engine that drove profit after all, and these guys could have borrowed fortunes. What a waste! If they knew what they were doing, they would pull that money out of their properties and make a ton more money.

But I'd lost my shirt, and here they were, making more money than ever.

The story of one lender I used to work with sums up the lesson I'm trying to impart quickly, though it took a crash and many years for me to learn. I would show up to meet this lender in my $105,000 Cadillac XLR convertible (man, I loved that car!), and he would show up in his nondescript Honda Accord. He was the lender, bringing me a check for $200,000 or $250,000 in what we call a "hard-money" deal, but I was the one driving the fancy car. I felt superior at the time, thinking, "This guy obviously doesn't know what he's doing."

The thing is, that Honda Accord was paid for, like all of this lender's properties. Most of what I "owned" wasn't. When the crash came, he didn't lose a single night's sleep. He continued to make money while I sweated bullets, robbing Peter to pay Paul and scrounging to hang onto whatever I could. Like that Cadillac convertible, my "empire" was a mirage. A house of cards.

Guess what kind of car I drive now?

Yes, I have a Honda Accord. That car is a symbol for me. And when people say, "When are you going to drive a car that matches your image?" I reply, "You clearly don't understand my image." I could now write a check for any car I wanted, but the Accord symbolizes my peace of mind and the idea of living within my means—more cash coming in than going out—thinking long-term, and building a passive income. It represents true wealth.

I learned from that lender who drove an Accord and from the other investors who thrived during the bust. After years of perfecting the slow flip, the bottom can fall out of the real estate market tomorrow, and I'll be just fine, too. In fact, I'll thrive, trawling for deals in my Honda and making the most of low prices.

Maybe there is no crash in the foreseeable future. In that case, wouldn't you still be in a better position and sleep more soundly if you owned some real estate free and clear? Wouldn't this be a good component of any investment strategy? What price would you put on peace of mind?

I valued security highly as I reevaluated my strategy post-crash. I took pieces from everyone I interviewed, assessed what I'd been doing well and poorly, and what I would change.

Meanwhile, housing prices kept tumbling, and as anyone who watched real estate would remember, it remained in the basement well past the official end of the recession, into 2011 and 2012. Here's a real-life example of the turn the market took.

I bought a house in Portsmouth, Virginia for $120,000. The lender gave me a loan for $150,000, so I put the excess, a check for $30,000 in my pocket, courtesy of the bank. The house was appraised at $199,000, so I felt like a superhero. I bought a house using someone else's money and left with a big check for more of their money. Who's smarter than I am?

Then came the bust.

The bank foreclosed on this house, along with many others. Through happenstance, I bought the same house back a few years later—the very same house, not a comparable one on the block. That same house, which I still own, sold for $30,000 after the crash. Think about this for a minute, the next time someone mentions the impressive assets they've assembled, what they're worth, and how they'll appreciate or hold their value. I buy a house that is appraised at $199,000, and I owe $150,000 on it, and later, I buy it back for $30,000 ultimately, a loss for me of $120,000. There are no guarantees, and leverage can make suckers of us all.

Buying that house back wasn't easy, by the way. As I mentioned, I'd lost most of my properties to foreclosure. Guess how good my credit was? By 2010, I couldn't have gotten a loan to open an ice cream stand in hell.

No bank would let me in the door, but I was able to find some private lenders eager to make loans and excited about bargain-basement housing prices. The challenge was that they all wanted to do deals like the banks and finance my purchases over 30 years. I'd bought cars for $60,000 to $70,000 and financed them over five years. I thought, "So, if I'm buying a house for $30,000, why stretch the payments over 30 years? Why not suffer through higher payments and no cash flow now and then own the house free and clear in five years? Why not put myself in the same comfortable position as my friend in the Honda Accord as soon as possible?"

This was a whole new mindset for me—suffer now and own sooner. By "suffer," I just mean forego cash flow in the short term to pay off properties quickly and then get paid, worry-free for the rest of my life. The spark that changed my thinking on this was the catalyst for everything we're going to go over with slow flips. I apologize for the biographical digression, but I wanted to share it so that you can understand why I changed, why I operate the way I do, and why I'll never go back to those high-anxiety, high-leverage days.

Getting to Freedom and Beyond

Fast forward, I've now been doing real estate full-time for more than 20 years. I've closed more than 800 deals, nearly all of them in my local market here, in Virginia. I now have 138 properties—all of them are slow flips. As I write this, I own 72 of those houses free and clear, and I have 20 deals under contract that I expect to close shortly. All these properties will be owned free and clear within five years because the way I do slow flips, five years is the maximum term for a loan.

I wanted to mention this number—138 properties, with 20 more in the pipeline—before we get to your future vision and what wealth means to you because my future vision called for fewer than 70 houses. That was all the passive income I needed to be comfortable. My "freedom number," as I like to say. So, why am I at double that number?

When I was getting close to 70 houses, I was at a ballgame, talking to one of my coaches, and mentioned that I was going to stop investing.

"What do you mean?" asked the coach. He was quite a bit older and always said he wished he'd had the opportunity to invest through slow flipping when he was younger (this is a guy who's been making other kinds of real estate investments for 50 years).

"I don't really need any more properties," I said. "Seventy is more than enough for my future vision. It's enough for everything."

"Keep buying," he said.

"Why?" I asked.

My coach pointed out that I didn't use any of my own money on these deals. That was true; I never used my money. He asked if these slow slips were taking up a lot of my time. "Almost no time at all," I said. He knew that I'd developed a system that pretty much ran itself (one I'll share with you in the coming chapters).

"So, you don't use your own money," he said. "They don't take up any time. They're readily available, and it's profitable. Why would you stop?"

I didn't think for long before agreeing that he was right (one of many examples, as we'll discuss later, of why it's vital that you have trusted people to discuss things with). I'm telling you this upfront because if you pursue slow flipping, you will likely be in that same position before long. We establish what wealth means for us and how we want to spend our days, and then, when we reach our individual freedom numbers, we have the option to keep going. Most people continue doing deals because, like me, they think, "Why not?" The point is it's your choice. You've hit your freedom number, realized your future vision, and achieved peace of mind. Everything else is gravy, and if you have a fairly automated system in place, why not scoop some more?

The most important number for me when I had that talk with my coach was not 70 or 138 but 12. This is the number of weeks I spend traveling with my family every year—a number and a goal that I took seriously when I started revamping my business full-throttle in 2011. I thought about how I wanted my life to look—12 weeks of family traveling time front and center—and what business would fit into the time left over. That's the opposite of what most people preach—work, work, work, then hope you have some time for family, your guitar, travel, cooking, whatever you're into before you die.

In my revamp, Scott 2.0, I made a strong effort to see and design my desired life. That was my starting point, and that's what I want readers to do—creating a future vision of the life you'd like to have.

We all think we want money, but as I mentioned in the introduction, money itself is useless. You actually want what money can buy you, and the thing most people want to buy with it is freedom. That is what you're working for.

Remembering that money is just the means to an end is important as you think about your future vision, your definition of true wealth, and how you want your life to look. Also, remember my cautionary tale about losing everything during the bust. If I'd taken the time to form a future vision before the boom and bust, I never would have participated.

I had 20 properties when the boom hit and probably owed $60,000 to $65,000 on each. Overnight, they were worth $150,000 to $160,000. I had plenty. It could have been a positive cash flow of $20,000 a month without participating in the boom. Instead, I did what society taught me to do. I pulled out the equity, and I bought more for the sake of more. I parlayed it all and subsequently, lost it all because I was unclear about my goals and what true wealth meant to me.

It's my mission here never to anyone force that model of blind consumption on you. If I'd spelled out how much I needed, what I wanted, and what my future vision looked like, I would have kept those 20 houses, collected $20,000 monthly, and ignored the gospel of leverage.

So, get out a pen and pad, and let's jot down why you're doing this. We're going to write down exactly what you need and want and then attach an amount to it, not the other way around. Some readers might be tempted to say, "Screw this! I want to make ten grand a month or $30,000 a month, but let's keep the horse solid before the cart."

I learned this lesson the hard way. When I could have been collecting $20,000 a month stress-free, I had another number in mind—$100,000 a month. Why? No reason whatsoever, except that it sounded like a nice round number. Hmm, 100k, that would mean I was rich, right?

What a mistake. I could have lived like a king on $20,000 a month. I could have stopped there, and in retrospect, I should have lived on $5,000 to $10,000 a month, parlayed that other $10,000 a month into building up to $30,000 a month, and grown incrementally, safely, from there.

So, I really want you to understand why you're investing. Give concrete answers—no vagueness—and write this down. Writing it down is vital!

Some of you have probably heard of the 1979 Harvard study in which researchers asked an entire graduating entire class which of them had clear, written goals. Only 3 percent of the students did. About 13 percent had goals, but they weren't written down, and 84 percent said, "*Nope, no goals. I'm here to party.*" Right? Their goal was just to graduate. Ten years later, researchers revisited the class. The 13 percent with unwritten goals earned about the same as the 84 percent with no clear goals. The 3 percent who'd written down clear goals earned ten times the amount of the other 97 percent "combined." Think about that. Yes, writing this down matters.

If you need more convincing, let me promise you that nothing you get trained on, no strategy or skill you pick up here, will be worth anything if you skip this first step. Your future vision is everything. It will guide all that you do and become your foundation, rudder, or compass ... Pick your favorite metaphor.

And it will only take a few minutes, so grab that pen and paper.

Form Your Future Vision

Think about what you want your life to look like and how you'd like to spend your days.

I'm going to give you a little guidance for this exercise. For starters, write it in the present tense, as if you were already living your desired future. We want it to feel real and achievable—it is! And putting it in the present tense will drive that point home, making the vision palpable. So, you'll write, "My day looks like this. When I get up in the morning, I get dressed, and then ..."

Writing out your future vision gives you a destination, but it also clarifies for your brain what's important and what you need to pay attention to on the journey to it. I'll give you an example of this dynamic.

Have you ever bought a new car? Let's say you're buying a bright blue Mustang convertible. On the way to the dealership, you're excited. You don't know a soul with this kind of car, so, boy, it is going to stand out. You buy the car, and cruising home on the highway, you see another bright blue Mustang convertible. That's weird. It must be the only other one for fifty miles. Two days later, you see another on your way to work. Pulling into your driveway the day after that, you notice that there's one car parked two houses down, the same bright blue Mustang convertible. Your neighbor owns the same car, and you never even noticed!

Here's another example of this dynamic that I experienced recently. I was leaving Best Buy when a guy stopped me.

"Hey Scott," he said, "You still buying houses?"

He obviously knew me. He said his name, and I made conversation, pretending to remember him, though I hadn't the foggiest.

When I got into my car, I typed his name into Facebook, and his profile popped up. Oh yeah, I'd met him a couple of years earlier after I spoke at an event. I remembered then that he was an entrepreneur and did Airbnb turnovers. I'd met him only once, so nothing strange about forgetting the face, right?

The strange thing is that when I went to the office the next day, his business card was sitting right in front of my keyboard on my desk. It has been there, ten inches from my nose, for two years. I never noticed it, saw it, or paid it any mind because it was irrelevant. The very next day after bumping into this guy, I noticed the card right away. Suddenly, it was relevant. It made the cut, and while my brain was filtering out endless other information, it knew to let this detail through.

This phenomenon occurs all the time, with everything you encounter. Your mind is overloaded every day, processing too many sensory details to absorb them all, but when something becomes important, you see it and remember it. You create a filter for your brain, clarifying what's important and should be let in. This is why it's important to write your future vision down. You're telling your brain in concrete terms what to look for as you go about your day.

Write your vision out like a child at Christmas. Don't worry about what's possible or feasible or what you think you can do. Write as if you can do anything, and failure is not possible. What would you do if you couldn't fail? What would you do if you only had six months to live? What would you want those last six months to look like? You weren't born to work and pay bills, so that you could get up the next morning to work and pay bills, then collapse, exhausted for a weekend before starting the cycle again.

You can be as ambitious as you like, but be specific and sincere too. Do not write down that you "want more" or wish for a certain dollar amount unconnected to the stuff you actually want. Be concrete. You'd like to pick a new country in Europe to spend a month in every year? Write it down. You'd like to spend half your week on the beach or a golf course, play competitive tennis, or send your kids to Princeton? Write it down.

It takes some effort for most people to create a genuine vision of how they want their days to look in the future because, in the present, their days and identities are inextricably tied to their jobs. Work hard at this vision. Before you put pen to paper, close your eyes for a minute and try to see your perfect day. I'm serious! Close them and see it.

How would your morning go? Where would you spend it, with who, and doing what? If you don't like the work you do now (most people don't), what sort of work would you like to do, if any? Do you picture yourself in an office with your own staff, wheeling and dealing; putting in time with a laptop at the cozy coffee shop on the corner; teaching underprivileged kids; or avoiding work altogether? Do you imagine yourself traveling to exotic locales, playing piano four hours a day, hitting all your favorite team's home games, training for a marathon, decorating a nice house, or owning a restaurant?

Remember, we are not worried about dollar amounts yet, just the stuff you want to do. Often, those things require much less income than people initially think they need. We're aiming for personal definitions of true wealth here, not fat bank accounts.

I'll tell a brief story that illustrates why this is so important. This fable exists in various forms, and many will have heard some version of it. I first read it in one of my favorite books, *The 4-Hour Workweek*.

An American businessman took a vacation to a small coastal Mexican village on Doctor's orders. Unable to sleep after an urgent phone call from the office on his first morning, he walked out to the pier to clear his head. A small boat carrying one fisherman and a massive yellow-fin tuna had just docked. The American complimented the Mexican on the quality of the enormous fish.

"How long did it take you to catch that?" he asked.

"A few hours; it was a good day," the fisherman replied in surprisingly clear English.

"Why didn't you stay out longer and catch more fish?" the American asked.

The fisherman shrugged. "I have enough to support my family and give some to friends," he said, unloading his haul.

"But what do you do with the rest of your time?"

The fisherman smiled. "I sleep late and play with my children, take a siesta with my wife, Julia, and in the evening, stroll into the village, where I sip wine and play guitar with my amigos."

"Look," the American said, "I have an MBA from Harvard, and I can help you. You should spend more time fishing and with the proceeds, buy a bigger boat. In no time, you'd be able to buy several boats with that larger catch. Eventually, you would have a whole fleet of fishing boats. Instead of selling your fish to a middleman, you could sell directly to consumers and down the road, open your own cannery. That way, you would control the product, processing, and distribution. You would need to leave this small fishing village, of course, and move to Mexico City, then to Los Angeles, and eventually, New York City, the center of finance. From there, you could run your expanding enterprise with proper management."

"How long would that take?" the fisherman asked.

"About 15 to 25 years," the American said. "But then, when the time was right, you would announce an IPO and sell your company stock to the public. You'd be rich! You could make millions."

"Then what?"

"Well," the American said, "You could retire to a small coastal fishing village where you would sleep late and play with your children, take a siesta with your wife in the afternoon, and in the evening, stroll into the village to sip wine and play guitar with your amigos."

Of course, our Mexican fisherman already had the result everyone is looking for. He was already living his ideal future vision. He had more coming in than going out, and he had all the stuff he wanted—true wealth. Focusing on some arbitrary dollar amount and conventional ideas of being "rich" couldn't make him any happier and probably would have made him miserable.

I thought of this fisherman fable over Christmas a few years ago on a family trip to Jamaica, where I encountered a real-life version. Our driver took us to this place called simply "the fishing beach," where his friends hung out. They caught all these great fish right there, scaled them over the water, and then threw them on a grill, right on the beach. It was unbelievably delicious, served with the cold beers they provided. We had an amazing time, and they charged us about $20 for the whole thing. We were a big group, and of course, I gave the guys a bunch more money.

My brother-in-law, who's something of a fish nerd, pointed to one of the fish that afternoon, and said, "Man, that's a parrotfish. It's worth $250. If only they knew what they were doing, they could make so much money."

His words made me think of the Mexican fisherman in the fable. These guys were hanging out on the beach, eating amazing fish, drinking cold beer, and smoking weed with friends. They were having the best days of their lives. How would having more money improve that? They knew exactly what they were doing. The people chasing more and more money, with no purpose are the ones who need help.

As you review your future vision, remember these happy fishermen! Make sure that the vision reflects what you really want, not what society or popular culture tells you to want. Think *ideal days*, not dollars. Once your vision is clear, future decisions become much easier. Faced with a tough choice, you can ask, will this bring me closer to the vision I have spelled out?

Calculate Monthly Costs

Now that you've formed a vision of the future you want, let's calculate what it costs. Look at the page containing your vision and put a number next to everything you can, a dollar amount. Make it a monthly number. What would it take you to live this life monthly? If you want to play 18 holes of golf every other weekend, with green fees and incidental costs, that might come to $200 a month. Put it down. If the annual Caribbean family vacation you're dreaming of will run in the neighborhood of six grand, budget $500 a month. Assign a monthly number to Suzy's private school tuition, car payments, sailboat, tennis lessons, and whatever you need to make the vision real.

Now, add those numbers up. The goal is to have a realistic estimate of the monthly income you need to live your future vision. Check the list over and make sure the numbers are as accurate as possible. Real monthly costs, no fudging! Why monthly? As a real estate investor, you must be able to think about everything in monthly terms—incoming cash, and outgoing expenses now and in the future. This is how the world works. Most bills, fees, and mortgage payments are figured monthly, including the payments you'll make and receive.

The monthly number you have arrived at is your freedom number. That's what you need coming in the door in passive income to realize your vision and live your ideal day over and over. This isn't to say that you won't earn more. As I mentioned, most people hit that number and feel secure, but realize they want to keep going. "Want" is the keyword there. Any work you decide to do at that point is your choice, like any hobby or personal passion because you don't "have" to do anything. Freedom and true wealth are about doing what we *want* to do and eliminating the things we *have* to do.

Your freedom number gets you to what I call "stress-free abundance." We all want abundance, but we forget about the stress that comes with what we imagine as abundant life. Do you really want to make a million dollars a year? That's a common wish, but for most people, it's a random number, unattached to the things they really value.

Earning a million dollars a year probably means you have 10 to 20 employees, a big overhead, an office, and all the attendant hassles. Would you rather have that or be debt free, owning a handful of properties that meet all of your actual needs?

Some people have expensive tastes and elaborate future visions. They want to race sailboats and tour the Greek isles in their own yacht. More power to them. They should work toward their high freedom numbers, but most of the students I work with arrive at much lower numbers after considering what their ideal days actually look like. The average in my experience is about $10,000 a month, and it doesn't take many slow flips to get there.

Depending on their particular situation, most of my students realize they can get to their freedom number with 10 or 20 slow flips; it rarely takes more than 30. You can enjoy an extremely nice life earning $10,000 to $20,000 a month. Again, most of them keep going beyond that amount. They enjoy the process and realize they can make more without much time or effort, so why not? The point is, with slow flipping, they get to that number and reach stress-free abundance in five years. Rentals and the typical BRRRR approach, which I've mentioned and will address in more depth later, might get you there in 30 years if there's no crash, you're still in business, and you haven't lost your sanity to three decades of hassles.

Share Your Vision

Once you've figured out your vision and written it down, share the current version with people. I say "current version" because it will change and grow as your conditions, goals, and ideas evolve. Your first reaction might be, "No way, I'm not sharing that. People will think I'm crazy!" "They're going to say, who do you think you are?" "I've been working at my job for 30 years, but you're going to live your ideal life in five?" "Do you think you're better than I am?"

Sure, you will hear these sorts of comments, but it's vitally important to share your vision anyway. Remember the story about buying a bright blue Mustang and my anecdote about bumping into that fellow at Best Buy? In each case, a kind of message was sent out to the universe that allowed someone to see relevant stuff that was previously invisible. It's as if your personal radar gets fine-tuned and starts filtering out all the garbage, to home in on things that really matter to you.

Once you put your vision on paper and begin sharing it with other people, opportunities will begin to pop up. For everyone who mocks your plan, someone else will see and share something that can help you realize your future vision. Just as I was shocked to see my Best Buy buddy's card right in front of my computer, you'll be amazed at the places where opportunities emerge.

We'll talk more about getting your message out there and cultivating opportunities in later chapters, but for now, let me say one more thing about the critics. Can you guess who your biggest detractors will be? A guy at one of my recent seminars had the answer when he said early on, "I hope this plan is good. I need to convince my wife."

Unfortunately, the toughest critics will be the people who are closest to you. That's just the way it goes, not necessarily your spouse, but it could be brothers, sisters, friends, coworkers, and close neighbors. If they're not on the same path you are, those closest to you will typically be the first to say, "*You can't do that. What makes you think you can set yourself free? What makes you special? That won't work! You can't do it.*"

At seminars, I often show an outdoor concert video that provides a good visual demonstration of the argument I'm trying to make. I can't show the video in a book, obviously, but I'll include a couple of screenshots to give you the basic idea (you can find the actual video online if you google "Sasquatch music festival dance video"). This has nothing to do with real estate specifically but applies to many facets of life. The first time I saw it, I thought, this is exactly what I've been telling people.

In the video, a young man was at the Sasquatch Music Festival in Washington State. He's way off to the side, all by himself, dancing his heart out on the lawn. His moves were bold, expressive, and some might say "out there." He got looks and headshakes and probably a few laughs from the people sitting closest to him and maybe some secret admiration.

None of it daunted him in any way. He kept doing his own thing, with energy and self-confidence. Despite the isolation—no one else near him was dancing—this is not a guy who worries about what people think.

After a couple of minutes, as you can see below, a guy in a green shirt ran across the field and joined him. He seemed to appear from nowhere, but he was attracted to this guy's energy and joined in the dance. The first guy was doing just fine, but having someone with him who gets it clearly gave him a burst of energy as they danced together. The people sitting nearby still weren't moving, joining in, or showing any enthusiasm. They were indifferent at best.

A minute later, a third guy showed up, also from way across the field. Like the second guy who joined in, he seemed to be saying, "You know what, I see where you're at with this. I believe in you, and I believe in your vision. I have a similar vision. Let's do this together." Again, there was a burst of energy, and the people sitting closest ignored it.

A few more people who get it came from across the field and joined in, and then a few more, all of them stepping over and flowing around the people sitting closest, frozen in place, like statues. Before long, the flow of people attracted to that little point of energy generated by one person doing his own thing became a massive wave. They streamed past the static people closest to the dancer until it seemed like half the audience—thousands of people—were clamoring to be a part of that vision generated by that one guy, who seemed like a weirdo at first. Now, he looks like a leader, a visionary.

This is how pursuing your future vision will go. Those closest to you, friends and family, are probably not going to catch fire. Some might believe in you or support you, but even if not a single one does, that's fine. Prepare yourself for their rejection and cynicism, and like the guy in our video, who started a movement, ignore it. Putting your message out there, announcing your future vision to the world, will draw believers. They'll come from far and wide like the people in the video, and they'll step over the detractors to help you. You have to have faith that people who get it will show up because if you stick to your plan, they will. To quote a more famous video, "If you build it, they will come."

Here's another way to think about this phenomenon: you are the average of the five people you spend the most time with. Some of you might have heard this idea, and I can tell you that it is utterly true. If you hang out with four people who make $30,000 a year, rest assured, you will make $30,000. If you hang around with a bunch of people who make $200,000 a year, you'll eventually make $200,000 or so annually.

I have lived this dynamic in ways good and bad, working at various jobs throughout my life. In addition, believe me, it's like an immutable law of physics. The law doesn't just apply to income, it's true of everything. If you think about your closest friends, the people you spend the most time with, you'll realize that you kind of dress alike. You end up liking the same shows, driving similar cars, and enjoying the same things because that's the way it goes for those social animals called humans. People tend to prefer and gravitate toward people like them.

Once you understand this law, you can harness it proactively. You can consider carefully whom you're going to spend your time with. Instead of thinking of your circle as random, put some effort into shaping it. Prioritize spending time with people who are on the same page as you and who have the same mission.

I've encouraged you to follow your vision and ignore the detractors, but if you hang out with a bunch of people who think you're crazy, eventually, they'll convince you that you are. The reverse is also true.

Hang out with believers, and you'll believe. I always tell people that if they are around me long enough, I'll convince them that they can achieve anything. That's just a part of who I am. It's why I love teaching and writing about real estate investing, and by picking up this book, you've already taken a step in the direction I'm nudging you. Whether you know it or not, the *Jelinek Effect* is already working on you!

The advice I'm giving you is sound, and I hope that based on the little bio I've given you on these pages or info that you found about me online, you know to take my counsel seriously because I have a proven track record. This is an important point related to the idea that you should hang around with people who get your vision: take advice only from people successful in the area they're advising you.

Sounds like common sense, I know, but you'd be amazed how many people are in the advice business, doling out wisdom on things they know little about. The greatest example of this is Oprah. I like Oprah, and I'm a fan of the empire she built, but I always find it laughable that she advises on marriage and parenting. People line up to take it, though she has never been married or had children.

If Oprah gives a seminar on building a brand or creating an empire, sign me up. There, she has a stellar track record, but in other areas, I'll look for tips from someone who has demonstrated success. Don't tell me how to treat my wife when you're on your fifth marriage or give me parenting advice when three of your kids are in jail. Sorry if this seems obvious, but many people will want to put their two cents in when they find out what you're doing, and it's important to ignore the ones who haven't been successful in real estate investing.

Action Steps

Before we move into the mechanics of slow flipping, here are some big-picture action steps you should take.

1. DROP YOUR LOSER FRIENDS

Sorry, I know this sounds harsh, and it doesn't mean that you can't ever hang with Dave the Downer or Negative Nancy, but if you're serious about realizing your future vision, you have to be intentional about who your pals and confidantes are. As we discussed, you are the average of the five people you spend the most time with. Do the math and choose them wisely. Your time is limited, and you want to surround yourself with as much positivity as you can.

2. CUT OUT THE NEWS

While surrounding yourself with positive people, you also want to cut the negativity feeding into your brain. The news filtering through TV, radio, newspapers, and endless websites is one of the biggest sources of negativity we encounter. There's little good on the news, almost by definition. I realize this advice seems odd but think of it as an experiment for the next month. You'll be amazed at how your life chugs along just fine without knowing what you're supposed to be afraid of tomorrow. Can you get through your day without hearing details of the latest mass shooting, health scare, or political brawl? Yup, and, in fact, you might find your mood improving and your days going better.

Will that leave you uninformed? On some things, sure. How many of them are important to your vision? Probably very few. I heard a quote a while back: *"If you don't watch the news, you're uninformed, and if you do watch the news, you're misinformed."* I choose to be uninformed, set goals, and wake up with purpose. Rise focused in the morning, knowing why you're getting out of bed and doing the things you do.

3. LIVE AT OR BELOW YOUR MEANS

This is one that people hate at my seminars. I came here to make money, they think, not learn how to live like a pauper. First, this doesn't mean living in poverty. It's actually the first step toward living with wealth, and then, you can set yourself free. The lower you make your monthly lease and bills, the quicker you'll be free.

Eliminating debt is a big part of living at or below your means. Think of debt as poison and try to get rid of it as quickly as you can. What about "good debt"—debt that's used to make money? Someone always asks this. Yes, I still go into debt. You have to go into debt in real estate. If you are going to college too, you'll go into debt for that education, but it's with the intent that the education will boost your income by some amount that will help you pay it off. When we buy a property, we get into debt, but we pay it off as quickly as possible. We can think of this sort of debt—the kind used to invest in an education or a property—as a necessary evil.

I think of even the most useful debt as necessary, not "good," and most debt is downright evil. As some readers probably know, debt is the most marketed product in America. If you haven't thought of it this way, know that debt is very much a product for those peddling it. Corporations spend more money on getting you into debt than they do selling you any other product or service.

A book I read one time suggested that when a consumer buys a new car and the paperwork is stamped "approved" or that credit card offer comes in the mail notifying you that you're "approved," substitute the word with "enslaved." What if instead of thinking, "Ah, great, I got this car, and I only owe $387 a month," you thought, "Okay, I just pre-sold some piece of my future life, and I'm now enslaved." I pre-sold X number of hours every month to generate the money to pay for something that's already in my possession.

I like to use Mr. Burns, the character from the cartoon TV show *The Simpsons*, to drive home the point. I picture him at the top of one of those tall bank buildings you see in major cities. He's sitting in a lavish office, rubbing his bony liver-spotted hands, and murmuring, "*eeeexcellent,*" in his most scheming, sinister tone. He's looking down at us with a cold grin, saying, "*Run along, all of you and keep making my money for me. Keep sending it right up here!*"

When you are in debt, you work to support that debt, slaving at the office, punching a clock at the plant, dealing with your tenants, fixing a broken air conditioner—all that effort just so you can write a check and send it up to Mr. Burns.

4. CREATE EXCESS INCOME

Step 4 is to create excess income. Simply put, you want an amount coming in that's higher than the amount going out; the cash you need to live your life and pay the bills. Don't ever let the incoming revenue reach parity with the outgoing, or even get close. Try to maintain a healthy buffer between expenses and income. The bigger, the better. This is closely related to the previous step, obviously, but my point there was more about reining in costs—at least in the short term—and avoiding debt. At the same time, we want to cultivate income streams that give us some security and begin to build wealth. We'll get into the specifics in the coming chapters.

5. INVEST AND REINVEST

This is where the magic happens, how we create real long-term wealth. Step 5 is a joy to work through. Now, you can give that money away, and it won't affect a thing. If a loan goes bad, it won't be a hardship. You can lend out your excess funds and multiply them or continue to do more slow flips and build a real empire. If you have an interest in rehabbing, wholesaling, or other strategies, you can pursue them. The point is, you're free, and everything you do is your choice. You've built a snowball that can't be stopped, and you're choosing which hills to roll it down. The rest of this book is about helping you get to Step 5.

Forgive the long lead-in, but after years of teaching, I'm convinced that investors need a firm foundation and a clear vision of where they're headed before taking a single step. Now, you're ready. In Chapter 2, we'll explore in more depth why slow flips are a faster and more secure path to true wealth than rentals. We'll bust what I call "the great rental myth" and get into the mechanics of slow flipping.

2

The Slow Flip Formula

Before we get into the mechanics of slow flipping and why it's the fastest possible path to true wealth in real estate, I'll explore why doing rentals the conventional way is not. You can achieve wealth with rentals, but for most, that comes 30 years down the road—if everything goes well and you weather the many risks and decades of stress. The idea that rentals are a fast path to wealth is a myth that we'll bust wide open here. In fact, rentals are a slow, risky path to wealth in some distant, theoretical future. Presently, they're a one-way ticket to an exhausting job working for Mr. Burns.

I'm starting with the great rental myth because I got burned for believing in it when I started. And that experience led me to a much safer and faster path to wealth. Slow flipping.

What do I mean by "the great rental myth?" Many readers have probably been fed this fairy tale in some form and learned its two big blind spots the hard way. The first problem with the conventional rental strategy is its endorsement of debt, an idea everyone teaches, as I mentioned in Chapter 1. The second is its rosy outlook on cash flow and maintenance costs. I've been to all the seminars and read all the books, and I'm going to explain why this standard investment wrap is deeply flawed in both areas.

Cash Model Vs. Leverage Model

Most real estate gurus tell you that if you have $100,000, you can buy one house free and clear (the cash model), or you can split that money up and buy 10 houses, putting $10,000 down on each and borrowing the rest (the leverage model). If the market appreciates by 10 percent, with the cash model, your house is now worth $110,000, and you make a 10 percent return. With the leverage model, you have 10 houses worth $110,000 each, so you make $100,000—a 100 percent return on your original investment. That seems like a pretty smart way to use your 100k, right?

Now, let's say you can charge $1,000 a month in rent for each house you buy. With the cash model—a single house you own free and clear—you collect $1,000 a month on your $100,000 investment. With the leverage model, you collect $10,000 a month—$1,000 for each of the 10 houses you bought. Of course, you have to make monthly payments on your 10 mortgages. For the sake of our example, we'll say those payments are about $800 each, $8,000 total each month for the 10 houses. Since you're collecting $10,000, that leaves you with $2,000 in monthly cash flow—double the amount of the cash model.

So, to recap, your equity goes up 100 percent with the leverage model, and you have a monthly cash flow of $2,000. With the cash model, your equity goes up just 10 percent, and you have a cash flow of $1,000 a month. This is an easy choice for the experts, as it was for me once upon a time. Leverage was the strategy everyone taught, as I've said, and I pursued it right up to the deadly cliff we call 2008.

Market Appreciation Cash vs. Leverage	Cash Model	Leverage Model
Original Investment	$100,000	$100,000
Houses Purchased	1 free & clear	10 mortgaged (10K down each)
10% Market Appreciation	+10% ($10,000 total)	+100% ($10,000 x 10 = $100,000 total)
Monthly Cash flow	$1,000	$2,000 (10k - 8k in mortgage payments)

What the experts don't tell you is that if the market drops by 10 percent—not impossible, believe me—with the cash model, you lose $10,000 in equity i.e. 10 percent of your original investment. You paid $100,000, and now, you have a property valued at $90,000. With the leverage model, you lose 100 percent of your investment. That's right, you have 10 houses worth $90,000 each, and you paid $100,000 each for them, so just as the $10,000 gain gets multiplied by 10 in the gurus' leverage model, so does a $10,000 loss. You still owe $90,000 on each of those 10 houses, and your original investment is simply gone. Poof!

Okay, you might think, "That second scenario is sobering, but markets fluctuate." If you're holding the properties and not selling, why would a drop of 10 percent matter? My strategy is long-term. Fine, but what if values drop by 30 percent? With the cash model, you have a house worth $70,000 that you paid $100,000 for. You've lost $30,000, and you still owe $90,000. That's $20,000 more than the house is worth. With the leverage model, you have 10 houses worth $70,000, and you paid $100,000 for each. You owe $900,000 for houses worth $700,000. You have lost your original investment, and you're $200,000 in the red. I can assure you that this is not a crazy hypothetical. I have lived through worse.

Market Appreciation Cash vs. Leverage	Cash Model	Leverage Model
Original Investment	$100,000	$100,000
Houses Purchased	1 free & clear	10 mortgaged ($10,000 down each)
10% Market Depreciation	-10% ($10,000 total)	-100% ($10,000 x 10 = $100,000)
Equity	$90,000	$0
30% Market Depreciation	-30% ($30,000 total)	-300% ($30,000 x 10 = $300,000)
Equity	$70,000	-$200,000

Again, you can say, "If I'm keeping the houses long-term and my tenants are making payments, who cares if the properties are negative or "underwater" (i.e., the loan principal is more than the home's value)?" That's a reasonable response, but what happens when your tenants don't pay? A precipitous drop in values could indicate recession, layoffs, or rising unemployment rates, so some tenants will likely get behind on rent. When times were good, you cleared $200 a month per house with the leverage model, collecting $1,000 in rent monthly and paying just

$800 per mortgage. Now, you're missing that $200 in cash for each deadbeat, and you have to come up with $800 for the bank out of pocket.

If three of your 10 tenants stop paying—a likely scenario if values drop 30 percent and unemployment rises—you now must find $2,400 each month in mortgage payments i.e. $800 x 3. You have $200 cash flow each month from the seven that are paying, but that adds up to only $1,400, leaving you in the hole by $1,000 a month. In case you think this is an unrealistic doomsday scenario, let me remind you that in the 2008 crash, many landlords would have been thrilled to have only a third of their tenants stop paying rent.

Don't Work for Mr. Burns!

The 2008 crash again? Poor Scott, some readers are thinking, "He has GRPTSD—Great Recession Post-Traumatic Stress Disorder. He's so scarred by that 2008 debacle; he can't think straight." "That kind of bust will never happen again." "For those who got into the market after 2012, values have only gone up." "That's a full decade of growth, so what's he worried about?"

Okay, let's say that the bust was a one-time deal. It'll never happen again. We'll focus instead on that $200 to $300 a month positive cash flow per house. That's a great return, right? The experts certainly think so. All of the books and seminars tell you to subtract your monthly mortgage payment from the rent you're collecting, to figure out your return. If you can generate $300 per house per month, that's phenomenal. Right? Multiply that cash by 12 months, and that's $3,600. Multiply that annual cash flow x 10 houses, and you're getting back about $36,000 on your $100,000 investment i.e. a 36 percent return. Who wouldn't want that?

For this scenario, we're assuming that every tenant pays. Let's leave out the possibility of a single deadbeat. The other thing we've been leaving out—an expense that must be included in even the rosiest projections—is maintenance. I have been in this business a long time, and I can tell you that the average house costs about $300 a month to maintain.

When I tell people this, they often laugh. *"I've had my property for two years,"* they say, *"and I haven't spent a single dollar on repairs,* or *"… I bought new construction, so I don't have to worry about repairs."*

I'm happy for you if you got away with no repairs for a year or two, but at some point, you will have a turnover. When tenants move out, you'll have to re-carpet and paint, minimally, before new tenants move in. Eventually, you'll have to replace the air conditioner. A new stove and refrigerator, at some point, will have to be bought. The roof that seemed perfectly sturdy will turn a corner after a couple of storms, and a new one will cost $8,000. An electrical or plumbing issue with a shocking price tag will arise.

If you track your numbers for two years, you might be perfectly fine. You can indeed go a year or two without repairs, maybe more if you're lucky. But think about the 10-year horizon. Things will wear out, and problems will emerge over a decade, even with new construction. You will be chugging along, in the black, happy with your return, and then, you'll be hit with a $1,000 turnover. One big repair, one stolen AC unit, or one year like 2020 in which a tenant stops paying and the government says you can't evict anyone, and you'll spend years catching up. Whatever money you thought you made will be gone in an instant.

"I can think long-term too," new landlords say. That's the whole point! "Sure, I might have a big repair and lose two years of cash flow, but then, I'll be ahead $200 a month the rest of the time." No, you won't. You're lying to yourself. The assumption is that maintenance costs will disappear after those two years, but more will pop up. And more and more, and then someone who seemed utterly trustworthy will trash one of your houses. A tenant you considered a friend will disappear, owing several months' rent ... You will spend the next 30 years chasing a profit, to no avail.

Thirty years is a long time, and what you'll come to realize over those decades of repairs, turnovers, cleanups, complaints, deadbeats, lawsuits, and evictions is that you have been working a job, a difficult, stressful one, at that. A 30-year mortgage is a *job*, and the minute you got that job, you became an employee. Do you know who your employer has been all that time? Have you guessed it? Yep, it's Mr. Burns.

Your job has been to handle all the headaches, heartaches, and stress for Mr. Burns, so he doesn't have to. When you finally get a check, you send it up to him. He's sitting in his corner office at the top of the bank building, rubbing those liver-spotted hands together gleefully as he counts your money. If a tenant skips out, a house is damaged, or a repair eats two years' profit, he doesn't care. Mr. Burns gets his, whether it comes from your tenants' pockets or yours. If a check doesn't appear, he takes the house back and sells it at a handsome profit, capitalizing on the equity you built for him. *Eeexcellent!*

This is the trap that most of the real estate experts out there writing books and holding seminars lead people into. I started teaching because I was shocked that after the crash, the gurus continued teaching the same strategy that made us stressed-out slaves in 2008. I had moved on to the slow flip, and I wanted to educate people about this other, less risky way to invest.

Essentially, slow flipping allows you to become Mr. Burns. It doesn't require sinister eyes or a bald head, and you don't need a corner office in the financial district, but it allows you to put deals together, and then sit back with your hand out to collect payments. No headaches, repairs, or long-term debt.

I wanted to present the typical real estate investment strategy that others teach so that I could highlight its inherent problems before explaining the ways we benefit by flipping the script. Hopefully, it's clear now that you want to be in the position of the lender, getting checks, not the landlord getting grief. The slow flip allows you to occupy that sweet spot, and in a moment, I'll explain the process step-by-step, using concrete examples.

As we explore the mechanics of slow flipping in the rest of this chapter, keep our friend Mr. Burns in front of mind. Every time you take on debt, sign on the dotted line, or mail in a credit card offer, you're taking a job with him. You're making Mr. Burns your boss, and he's no fun to work for. This is also true of financing cars—don't do it!—and of going negative on properties (i.e., paying more for mortgages and maintenance than you collect in rent).

It's okay to break even monthly. My business plan actually calls for that for the first five years, but you never want to be negative. Operating properties in the red monthly will make you miserable as you work long hours at another job to pay for your real estate business. It also puts you at risk. You want to breathe easily while you invest and build wealth. Running negative each month puts you on a tightrope, and the smallest financial setback can knock you off.

At the end of Chapter 1, I suggested that every time you see the word "approved," you should mentally replace it with "enslaved" to see debt in the proper light. Another helpful way to think of it is that when you take on debt, you're preselling your future. If you make $10 an hour and take out a car loan with payments of $200 a month, you just presold 20 hours of your month for years to come. If your house payment is $1,000 a month, you have presold 100 hours. Every time you charge up your credit card, take a vacation, or go out to dinner, you're preselling another 30, 40, or 50 hours of your month.

Eventually, no time remains. You have presold it all, and you must work long hours just to pay for what you already possess (I don't say "own" because, technically, Mr. Burns owns it; you're just keeping it warm for him). This is when they have you. It's what we mean by the "rat race," spinning furiously on an economic hamster wheel, with no way to get ahead. Mr. Burns owns what you possess, and in a sense, he owns you.

I'm giving you another rant about debt because slow flipping does require borrowing, and I want you always to be wary about how much you borrow and for how long. As I said in Chapter 1, debt is never good, but it is sometimes necessary. In our system of slow flipping, we strive to keep the amount of debt low and the repayment term as short as possible.

Some readers might be familiar with investment guru Dave Ramsey, who preaches avoidance of all debt except when it comes to the house you live in. I applaud his wariness of debt, but if you took his advice, you would never buy properties until you saved up enough to pay cash for them. Even with great jobs and incredible discipline, most people would be lucky to swing two or three houses over a lifetime that way. It's the opposite extreme of the leverage argument—a formula for keeping your head above water, not for living a better life.

Our slow flip system takes a middle path. Yes, debt is bad, and the gospel of high leverage is poison, but we do need to borrow as investors. Loans are okay as long as we think of debt as a necessary evil, keep the amount small, and pay borrowed money back as quickly as possible. Our time horizon on borrowing for a slow flip is five years max—same for a car—not 30, like the typical house.

The Slow Flip Defined

In the introduction, I gave you my general definition of a slow flip: *the process of flipping a property as slowly as possible for the fastest path to wealth.*

Let me reiterate that slow flipping is not the fastest possible path to a check or a fat bank account. Rehabbing and wholesaling will put $30,000 to $50,000 checks in your account faster, and I'm not opposed to those pursuits if you want to try them. I personally love wholesaling and still do it, but wholesaling and rehabbing are not about wealth as I define it.

I think of wealth as passive income—more money coming in than going out, not just for a month or a year, but permanently, without having to work for it. Wealth means I have enough to pay all my bills and something left over every month, every year. How much is that? The answer will be different for every reader, which is why we devoted Chapter 1 to finding your number and defining what true wealth means for you.

I recently coached a student who figured that all he needed to take care of his wants and pay every bill was $2,000 a month. That's an unusually low amount, but I was excited about it. Wow, we can get you there really quickly, and we did. He might not be wealthy now, according to conventional standards, but he is free. He reached his "freedom number," and if he chooses to, he can keep building from there with additional slow flips.

I'll give the general steps involved in slow flipping below, and then explore each in detail. In slow flipping, as I've said, we buy distressed houses for cheap, using private money with a five-year term. We then sell the houses "as is" at a hefty markup, with long-term owner financing. In five years, you own the house free and clear, but the buyers, who have a 30-year term, keep paying you. Do a few of these, and you start to build a nice, steady income stream for the long haul.

You essentially act as a bank in a slow flip, putting the deal together by finding private money, finding and purchasing a house, and then, finding a buyer to sell it to. You're creating value and earning money the same way Mr. Burns does.

One of the many advantages of this process is that you are not a landlord. I have been a landlord many times over, so trust me, when I tell you that it sucks. Collecting rent, fixing stopped-up toilets, cleaning trashed houses, fielding midnight calls when pipes burst, or being sued; none of this is fun. With a slow flip, you turn the house over to a purchaser who has all the responsibilities of ownership. If your buyer doesn't like the living room's colors, she can repaint. If someone smells gas at 2 a.m., it's his job to call the gas company. It's your job to collect checks once the deal is done. That's it.

Most people think of rehabbing when they hear the word "flip" in real estate, and one standard model would be to renovate the houses you buy before selling them. Another advantage of the slow flip model is that we sell "as is," with no rehabs or even cleanup. Rehabbing is expensive, difficult, and time-consuming, and even if you are into construction, a lot can go wrong. We are operating at a price point where no one expects Buckingham Palace, and buyers are happy to purchase a modest house "as is" with low money down and manageable monthly payments.

I hope that you're starting to get a feel for how the process works, but to make sure, I'll give a quick step-by-step overview before we go into more detail about various parts of the slow flip.

1. **Access private money.** We get funds not from professional lenders but from ordinary people who have some money to spare and are tired of the miserable returns they earn at the bank or the fluctuations of the stock market. There is an enormous amount of such money out there, and I'll help you find it. You don't need good credit or collateral (other than the houses you're purchasing). Private money comes at a higher interest rate, but

we don't mind that because we're borrowing a comparatively small amount and paying it off quickly, within five years.

2. **Buy**. Find and purchase a distressed house for around $30,000. We are looking for motivated sellers in Step 2, so we can buy well below market value. Some homeowners need to dispose of houses quickly. Maybe the home is in bad shape, and its owners can no longer pay the taxes, much less fix it up. There might have been a death in the family, job loss, a difficult divorce, or major medical debt. Some sellers want to skip the hassles of brokers and marketing, and they'll take a low price from someone who offers a quick, clean exit. Such homes exist in nearly all areas, as we'll see, though not necessarily at the $30,000 price point. If you're in a pricey area, you can slow flip in other more affordable locations, as I'll explain shortly.

3. **Sell.** Put the house on the market immediately. We sell the house "as is" at a hefty markup. I typically pay $30,000 for my houses, as I said, and my average sales price is $89,000. I will explain later why I like these numbers (for starters, they work). We sell with "long-term owner financing." This simply means that a buyer purchases the house with $3,000 to $5,000 down and a monthly payment to you over 30 years (you're the bank). That payment covers your payback to the private-money lender for the next five years, as well as taxes and insurance.

4. **Cash checks.** The amount you collect covers your payments to your lender plus taxes and insurance for five years, so you break even until your loan is paid. After five years, you own the house

free and clear. Checks from your buyer now go into your pocket. If buyers remain for 30 years (almost no one ever does), you collect ten times your original investment. If they sell the house or give it back, you have an $80,000 house you paid $30,000 for and can use that money to do more slow flips.

My Formula for Buying

You need money to buy houses, obviously, but I'm going to hold off on Step 1 above—accessing private money—because I'll devote all of Chapter 5 to it. First, let's talk about my standard formula for buying. It's not set in stone, and I'll discuss possible variations, but I've come to this model after years of trial and error. I know that it works, and while there is some wiggle room depending on circumstances, I recommend following this template as closely as you can, especially when you're starting.

I try to keep my acquisition costs at $30,000 per house with slow flips. This is the sweet spot I've arrived at, after many years of buying and selling. I've done enough seminars to know that two big questions will spring to mind for savvy readers. The first relates to the availability of houses at this price point and the second to current market conditions.

Let's tackle the $30,000 question first. Some readers right now are saying to themselves, "Scott is out of his mind. There aren't any houses for $30,000." I have a previous book that got just one negative review on Amazon, a comment saying that I was crazy for thinking houses could be found for $30,000.

Well, I'm here to tell you that, "Yes, in fact, you can find houses for $30,000 and less." There is an abundance of them. Now, they might not be available in your market. If you live in California, Seattle, Manhattan, or Washington DC, it's a tall order. There are many markets where you can't buy a house for $30,000, but typically, they can be found within three to five hours of wherever you live.

Not only is there usually a close market where you can buy them, but they're also probably plentiful there. When you hear $30,000 house, some of you might be picturing four sheets of plywood and a tarp roof, but I can also tell you that the quality of houses a smart buyer can find for this price will surprise you. I'll print photos of some of my own properties bought for $30,000 or less in these pages, including the most derelict house I ever purchased, and explain how they worked out.

The second likely question is, how given market conditions at the time I'm writing this relates to price fluctuations. In late 2022, the real estate market is very good, which has affected our $30,000 target. As the year wraps up, I have students who can pay up to $50,000 for slow flips, still finance them with five-year private-money loans, and make the deals work. Rising rents and market pressure have increased what people are willing to pay per month, so my students can still pay off their lenders in five years.

I'm telling you that this higher price point in the late 2022 market is possible, but I'm not encouraging you to base your plans on it. I don't teach my model using these higher prices because we don't know how long current market conditions will last. By the time this book is printed and distributed and finds its way into your hands, the market might already have shifted to make those $50,000 houses untenable.

The formula can be altered on a case-by-case basis for changing market conditions and what I call unconventional slow flips. One of my students just did a deal in which he paid $175,000 for a six-plex, for example, and was able to slow flip it. I recently slow flipped an 8,000-square-foot commercial building. It turned out to be one of the best deals I've ever done, but it's atypical and not the kind of transaction we're focusing on here.

My point is that the formula I'm teaching you can be modified, but we really want to buy houses for $30,000 or less. Stick with the formula as you're starting because we know these numbers work.

I borrow $30,000 at 12 percent to purchase a house on my slow flips. As I've said, you don't need any of your own money to pursue slow flipping. You're using private money to buy the house. We'll explore private money in depth in Chapter 5, as I mentioned, but I want to say here that I borrow the full $30,000 at 12 percent on every single deal, even if the home price is under $30,000.

Why borrow more than you need—the full $30,000, even if the house costs $25,000 or $15,000? The answer is that you are cultivating, or we might even say "training," your lenders. Just as there is value for you in following a formula, they'll appreciate the familiarity and consistency of your unwavering numbers.

But if on one deal, you borrow $15,000 and on the next, $40,000, your lenders will start comparing. Maybe you get a really good deal on a $15,000 house they loaned you the money to buy. The next one you want to purchase is $30,000. The same lender looks at that house and thinks, "Well, this isn't twice as nice as the one I loaned $15,000 on, so why would I loan $30,000 for it?" Soon, they'll be comparing every property to previous deals and cherry-picking the ones they want to finance.

I've established that, across the board. I borrow $30,000 for every deal, regardless of what I pay for a house. If I buy one for $35,000, I bring the difference, $5,000. If I buy one for $20,000, I pocket the difference, $10,000. My lenders know that when Scott comes knocking, he borrows X, and we are paid Y. The return is good; the numbers never vary, and for them, you start to look like a sure thing. This is your program, and following the formula puts you in control

I know that some of you are wondering, why $30,000? Why not $35,000 or $50,000? I settled on $30,000 after years in the business because the numbers work well. You can vary the interest rate to whatever is best for you and your lenders, but for me, $30,000 at 12 percent means my payment to my lender is $667 for the next five years.

Think about this. What you have here is, basically, a car payment. There is comfort in the formula for my lender, but also for me. My interest rate of 12 percent sounds quite high (more on this rate in Chapter 5), but that's not the important number. What matters is that I'm buying a house with a mortgage payment of $667.33 for 60 months, just as I would buy a car. I'm going to collect payment from my buyers of at least $875 a month, so I won't be making money for five years, but I'll be in a comfortable position. For 60 months, I have had the equivalent of a car payment. On the 61st month, I have no payment. I own a house free and clear, and I put the payment that my buyers send me in my pocket.

There is room for variation, as we've seen, but I want you to focus on $30,000 and the corresponding monthly payment. The math gets more complicated, and your comfort level can diminish if you're buying at higher prices.

My Formula for Selling

One reason that the purchase price of $30,000, or less, works so well is that I sell my houses for an average of $89,000 on a slow flip. We'll do the math on this shortly, but that sales price means I'm collecting on average $875 a month. This has gone up in the hot market we're experiencing as I write this, but again, I don't want to base anything on what might be a temporary state of affairs. Sticking with the numbers I've consistently used for years—collecting $875 a month from your buyer to pay off $667.33 for 5 years—puts you in a comfortable zone. It lets you pay off a house just as you would a car, over 60 months.

The difference between the monthly amount you collect and the amount you pay your lender on a $30,000 house—$207.67, for anyone without a calculator handy—covers taxes and insurance, with maybe some change left over. Essentially, we're breaking even for five years. If I pay more than $30,000 for the house and my mortgage payment goes up by, say, $300 a month, then I'm negative. Well, you might think, "If I'm negative by just $90 or so, that's not a big deal. I'll make up the difference.

Don't do it!

As we discussed earlier, paying more than you're collecting on a slow flip will make you miserable as you work long hours at a day job to subsidize your real estate investing. The idea is to reduce stress about bills, not add to it. Going negative also puts you at risk, and the whole point here is to minimize risk.

Slow Flip Formula	You	Your Buyer
Purchase Price	$30,000	$89,000
Loan Term	5 years	30 years
Monthly Payment for 1st 5 Years	$667.33	$875
Monthly Payment for the next 25 Years	$0	$875

It is okay to break even, and with the slow flip, we're basically breaking even for the first five years. The payment we collect covers the payment we make to a private-money lender, with little left over after taxes and insurance, so we want to start being paid as soon as possible.

If I buy a property today for $30,000, I will immediately put it up for sale, this afternoon or tomorrow. I want to start collecting payment from a buyer as soon as possible, and I can look for one immediately because I'm not improving the property in any way. I don't paint it, sweep rat poop, clean, or mow the lawn. I'll explain shortly how we turn not improving the property into a plus for buyers.

I typically sell the house for $69,000 to $99,000. Over the years, my average has consistently been $89,000. As I write this, I'm often getting

$119,000 to $129,000, but again, I don't want you to model on these numbers because we don't know how long they'll last.

How do I structure the sale? Usually, I take a down payment of $3,000 to $5,000. Sometimes, if the house is very dilapidated and needs major work, I'll go as low as $2,000 down. In the current fast-paced real estate market, I'm often getting $8,000 to $10,000 down for the same quality houses. It's not unusual in today's market to buy a house for $20,000 in a slow flip, and then sell it for $8,000 down and a monthly payment of $1,175. But we're in a strange time, and it's safer to stick with the more conservative numbers.

What I want to emphasize here, as I hope you can see from the chart above, is that you're breaking even for five years. You're paying $667 a month to your lender and collecting $875, but the difference between those payments mostly goes to escrow for taxes and insurance. The chart below lays out the structure of owner financing, which puts you in the role of Mr. Burns.

Owner Financing	Sale Price	Down Payment	Buyer's Payment	Term	Principal & Interest paid over 30 Years
	$89,000	$3,000–$5,000	$875 monthly	30 Years	$315,000

We'll get to amortization and the way mortgages work in a moment, but for now, just consider how sweet it is to be Mr. Burns. Because you're providing the financing for the purchase, your buyers would pay you $315,000 for an $89,000 house over 30 years if they stayed in it (virtually no one does for the full 30 years). What's more, is that you only paid $30,000 for the property. Where is all the extra money coming from?

This is the magic of financing. You're buying the home on a five-year mortgage and selling it on a 30-year mortgage. Essentially, you buy the house like a car and sell it like a house. Your suffering (which isn't really suffering; it simply means breaking even) lasts five years. Your buyers' suffering (which isn't really suffering either, since they're able to buy a house with poor credit and a low down payment) lasts up to 30 years.

The gap between what your buyer pays you and what you pay your lender is huge and in some sense, imaginary, just that the gap between your purchase price and your selling price is the value created out of thin air. It's the same house, the exact same as the day you bought it, so all this other money is simply made up. Right?

In a way, this increased "value" is imaginary, but the monthly payments are not. Those are real, and they add up. Buyers are paying you real money toward that invented price, and they're paying significant interest on it. This is how banks make their money, broadly speaking, and if you've ever gotten an auto or home loan, you know that you were willing to pay a premium to get the keys to a nice new vehicle or a house that you could say you bought and would be able to change any way you wanted. Something you can't do with a rental. Theoretically, you can sell it yourself someday and make money on the equity you've built up.

As a real estate investor, you find a house at a low price in a slow flip, and you arrange the financing that will allow someone who might have poor credit or a spotty job history to enjoy the benefits of homeownership. There is real worth in that. You are creating true value and a real opportunity for someone. They wouldn't pay you otherwise.

Remember that you are not just selling the house but first, the financing itself. You found the house, created the whole process, and created the note (the legal document setting out mortgage terms). If you bought a house for $30,000 in Indiana and tried to sell it for cash, unimproved, the next day, you'd probably get close to the $30,000 you paid. But you're not selling it for cash. You are providing financing, a mechanism that allows more people to buy, including people who can't get bank loans. The opportunity you're creating has real value, with a real dollar amount attached to it. This is how you create money.

At this point, students are often skeptical that anyone will pay $80,000 today for the house I bought for $30,000 yesterday. Why wouldn't they go find their own $30,000 house? I mentioned this in the introduction, and we'll address it in more depth later, but I want to touch on it here too since it's related to the idea of creating value.

When you buy a distressed house for $30,000, you must arrive with a check for $30,000. That's what makes the deal work, and it's a big part of why you can buy the house at a discount. Someone wants out as soon as possible. They don't want to mess with real estate brokers, banks, and marketing. You bring cash and offer them a quick, easy exit.

Your potential buyers don't have this ability. They can't raise private money and perhaps have never even considered the concept. They also, in many cases, can't swing a traditional bank loan. This is why they can't purchase the house that you can for $30,000 in cash and why they're happy to buy it from you at a price that's a significant markup but will still seem reasonable to them and is reasonable in market terms. The numbers they're concerned about are $3,000 down and $875 a month. They can manage that, and paying it will make them homeowners.

Sometimes, my buyers aren't even aware of the actual sales price until they look over the paperwork. They saw a house advertised for $3,000 down and $875 a month. We get to the paperwork, and they see a sales price of $80,000 and say, "This seems high. I saw one for sale down the block for $40,000."

My response to this is always the same, "Well, $40,000 does seem like a really good deal. I would buy that one if I were you."

"But I spoke to that owner, he said, and on that one, you have to pay cash."

"Hmm," I'll reply, "then, maybe you should buy mine since you don't have that kind of cash and you don't need cash for this purchase."

I simply put the option back in the buyers' hands. We don't hide anything or pressure anyone. If you can make that $40,000 house work with cash; obviously, that's the way to go. You don't have $40,000 and can't obtain it quickly? Okay, if you want to, you can buy my house for $3,000 down and $875 a month, no credit check, and no job check. I'll finance it for you. Think about it. If you decide you don't want to buy my house, you can always keep renting.

Interest Rates: Amortization

This is the short answer to the question of why your buyers would pay your asking price: because they can.

The next question that smart students and buyers ask now is usually, what is the interest rate? I have left the interest rate out of our formula until now because, from our perspective as investors, the down payment and monthly payment are what matter, just as they are the most important elements for buyers. We think about the monthly payment first and then back our way into an interest rate, figuring it out on one of the many amortization apps available. Just type "amortization calculator" into your app store or web browser, and you'll see many free options.

I just now pulled up one of these calculators for a hypothetical house. I slow flip for $89,000, and I will show the results below. I type in the price, $89,000, as well as $3,000 for a down payment and a term of 360 months or 30 years. I leave the interest rate blank but type in whatever monthly payment my buyers and I agreed to, in this case, $875. I hit enter, and ... I get an interest rate of 11.81 percent.

Sales price	Down Payment	Loan Amount	Monthly Payment	Term	**Interest Rate**
$89,000	$3,000	$86,000	$875	30 years	**11.81%**

We always make our calculations in reverse on a slow flip because we're most concerned with that monthly payment. It must cover our monthly payment to our private-money lender, as well as taxes and insurance. We want to at least break even for five years and then keep the checks flowing for the next 25 years while we put them in our pockets. We'll charge whatever interest rate corresponds to the monthly payment we need to make the slow flip work, given a specified down payment and sales price. The interest rate can fluctuate depending on the deal and the specific numbers agreed to.

Sometimes, for example, buyers fixate on the sales price. They don't want to pay $89,000, but they're willing to pay $86,000. That's fine with me, as long as I receive my necessary monthly payment. I can't budge on the $875 a month because I am not willing to go negative. I punch the new sales price into my amortization calculator, along with the same monthly payment and down payment, and I get a new, higher interest rate. The buyers are satisfied even though, as I make clear, they will be paying the exact same amount. They will make the same monthly payments and pay the same amount over a year, the exact same whole amount for the house over time.

The math there doesn't make much sense, but you'll find buyers with some psychological block about paying more than a certain "price," and we're happy to accommodate them. Just remember, we do not budge on the monthly payment we're collecting. The slow flip rests on that solid foundation.

The slow flip also relies on "amortization," which I've mentioned several times. It's a word that any reader who has ever purchased a house knows all too well. Simply put, amortization refers to the monthly schedule according to which you pay principal and interest on a loan over time. If you don't know this already, you won't be shocked to learn that amortization works heavily in Mr. Burns' favor (of course, it does. He and his fellow bankers invented it!).

Early on, when you're repaying a loan, the vast bulk of your payment goes toward interest (the rate charged for borrowing), and very little comes off the principal (the actual amount borrowed). Later, more of your payment applies to the principal and less to interest. Mr. Burns is paid first, which sucks when you're a homebuyer but is comforting when you become Mr. Burns in a slow flip.

Borrowing money to purchase a home is expensive, even when conventional interest rates are good, which is why you get paid handsomely for financing a home in a slow flip. Your buyers have to pay you $875 for 360 months, or 30 years before they own the house free and clear. What do those payments add up to? If you don't have a calculator handy, I'll tell you that it's $315,000. You paid $30,000 for the house, and if your buyers go the distance, you collect $315,000 in monthly payments, plus the down payment, before they own it. Not a bad return, right?

This is simply how mortgages work. The person or institution providing the financing is paid very well and is paid first. Anyone who owns a house knows this, though first-time homebuyers are often shocked to see the accounting system in practice. If you buy a house for $100,000 and send in your first check for, let's say, $1,000, you feel good about it. We're that much closer to owning this free and clear! Except when you look at the statement, only $30 or so came off the principal. The rest, $970, was applied to interest and pocketed by Mr. Burns. This is how over 30 years; we get up to $315,000 on our model slow flip.

I will punch the numbers for a recent slow-flip scenario into the first mortgage calculator that pops up on my browser and print the results below to give you a concrete look at amortization. In this example, I bought the house for $30,000 and sold it for $93,000, with a $4,000 down payment, so the loan amount was $89,000. Over 30 years, payments of $875 a month on that $89,000 loan work out to an interest rate of about 11.4 percent. If repayment started in January of 2023, the buyers' first check would pay about $29 off the principal and $845.50 in interest. For that entire first year, my buyers would only have paid only $335.46 off the loan principal of $89,000, the amount they're borrowing from me. The rest of what they paid me that year, a total of $9,284.87, was all interest.

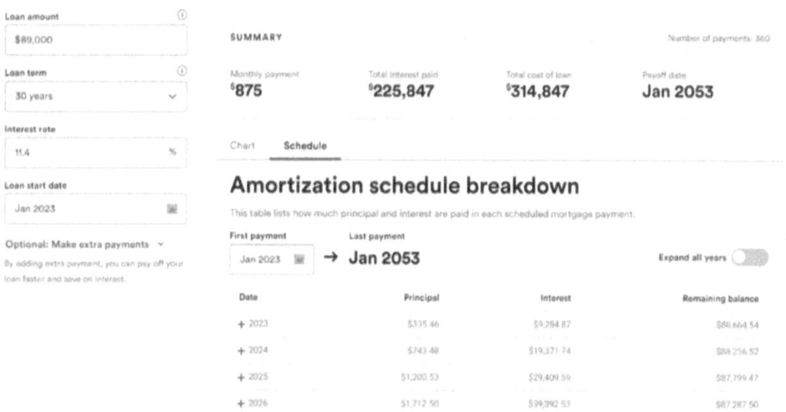

In year 10, as you can see below, my buyers have only paid about $6,300 off the principal and nearly $98,000—more than the value of the house—in interest. They still owe $82,631.88 on the $89,000 loan after a decade of payments.

Amortization Year 10	Principal Paid	Interest Paid	Remaining Balance
2032	$6,368.12	$97,706.31	$82,631.88

This might seem like a legal robbery; it's certainly a very good deal for lenders, but we didn't invent the system. This is simply how loans work. Many buyers figure they would spend a similar amount on rent over a decade, build zero in equity, and have no ability to change the property they live in, so despite the money poured into interest, buying still seems like a good deal.

How many buyers will stay the course for 30 years and pay the loan back in full? Probably none. Statistically speaking, the average American of prime home-buying age moves about every three to five years. That's a lot, right? It sounds crazy to me. I was in my last house for 16 years, and I'll stay in my current house until I die, but the odds are that your buyers will move within that short time frame. When that happens, they will either give you the house back, sell it to a new buyer, or operate it as a rental themselves.

Whatever your buyers do, you win. If by some chance, they stay for 30 years, you collect $315,000 on a house you paid $30,000 for. If they sell the house to a new buyer, you get $80,000, a 267 percent return. When you are paid off, you can use the money to buy more houses and do more slow flips. Should your buyer move but keep the house to operate as a rental, you continue to collect your payments and they deal with the headaches of being landlords.

My standard model is to use private money to finance slow flips, but if a pile of cash is simply sitting in a bank account making a poor return, why not use it to buy a house? By saving the interest you would typically pay a private-money lender, you're making a guaranteed 12 percent return right off the bat.

Your Slow Flip Number

You now have a model for the slow flip and how it works. We've covered the formulas for buying, selling, and amortization. And we've explained how you're creating value out of thin air by arranging the financing for people who might not otherwise be able to buy property.

We are going to dig deeper into the mechanics of slow flipping in a moment, but before we do, I want to revisit the "freedom number" you came up with in Chapter 1. Remember your future vision, which you wrote down and then converted into a dollar amount. I have helped many students calculate this personal number over the years, so I know that for many readers, it is between $5,000 and $10,000. Some have numbers in the range of $20,000, and a handful of readers might have numbers as high as $50,000 or $75,000. If your genuine number defining what true wealth means for you is quite high, that's perfectly fine, but you'll have some extra work to do.

Most people who start with very high numbers realize that the things they really want daily cost less than the amount in their heads, and numbers shrink as the vision clarifies. Some remain high.

Whatever your freedom number is, divide it by 500. This is the number of slow flips you need to realize your vision. Why 500? In slow flipping, we calculate that we're making about $500 per property per month. Your tenant pays you $875 each month. In five years, those checks are yours, but you've to pay off your lender, and you still have to pay taxes and insurance from them. Pay those bills, and you're probably left with closer to $650, but out of caution and for the sake of round numbers, we call it $500.

This means that if you need $5,000 a month to realize your vision, you need 10 slow flips.

$5,000 Income ÷ $500 Per Property = 10 Slow Flips.

If you need $10,000 for your vision, you need to do 20 slow flips. Note that the numbers of slow flips necessary for these dollar amounts—a range that probably covers most readers' goals—are not high. They are utterly attainable. With just 10 to 20 slow flips, most readers can realize their visions and begin living the lives they were meant to live. After notching 10, 15, or 20 of these deals, you can wake up in the morning and do exactly what you want. You can make the ideal days that we explored in Chapter 1 a reality. These are not lofty or unrealistic goals, by any means.

I have students, real estate novices, who have done 22 and 23 slow flips in one year. This means that even those readers with much higher ambitions—$25,000 or $50,000 in monthly income—have a practical path to get there. In my experience, as I've said, most people with high numbers tend to revise downward as they consider what they really want. Conversely, most of those with modest freedom numbers reach them and then keep going. Once investors are secure and know the ropes, why not forge ahead?

Of course, you don't attain freedom when you hit your goal of 10 or 20 done deals. The payoff comes five years after you reach your requisite number of slow-flip houses. In a way, we're on an accelerated, smarter, safer version of my "McDonald's Plan," which I described in Chapter 1:

buy a bunch of houses with high leverage and no financial buffer, and then wait 30 years. We use sound numbers and suffer now—no cash flow—to pay these houses off in five years. That's when the checks start rolling in. You hit your number and realize your vision. That's when you begin living your ideal days and can decide if you want to keep going. Most people do, but it's your choice. The only work you *have* to do at that point is cash checks.

You now have the big picture. You know where you're going. Your destination is that future vision you took the time to shape, assign a dollar amount to, and then translate into slow flips. However many slow flips you need to get to freedom—5, 10, 20, or more—you understand in general terms how they work: we buy properties like cars and sell them like houses for long-term passive wealth.

But how do you get started? How do you find the houses in the $30,000 range that are obviously the key to slow flipping? In Chapter 3, I'll present a variety of concrete strategies for discovering deals that will allow you to get started and hit the ground running.

3

Finding Slow Flips

When I coach students, which I've done on a limited one-on-one basis for years, I give them 47 different techniques to find deals and motivated sellers. In the interests of space here, I'll narrow those strategies down to the ones that are most relevant and effective for slow flips since that's our focus. Before we get to concrete strategies, let's talk about why the deals that we're hunting for exist in the first place.

Real Estate Purgatory

Our motivated sellers live in what I call real estate purgatory. Their houses are stuck in the middle, unwanted, and unloved. The houses haven't been condemned, demolished, or taken back by lenders, but they're often in poor condition. The homeowners are generally having a tough time too. They would like to sell but don't have the wherewithal to fix and clean up their houses for a regular marketing campaign, with a real estate agent showing the property. They might also be pressed for time and cash and don't want to spend months, a year, or more selling the property.

A rehabber might provide a good exit, but conventional flippers and rehabbers don't want these places because they have low ARVs. That stands for After-Repair Value, and it's a key number for rehabbers.

Rehabbers and most flippers (the kind who turn properties over quickly) want to go in, do some improvements—many of them cosmetic—and then sell the house at a profit. They are adding value by making some basic repairs and making the house presentable. They aim for houses with high potential ARV.

The typical slow flip house is more work than a rehabber wants. It's often a mess and not worth the investment of time, energy, and money it would take to renovate. Such a house is impossible to get a mortgage on in its current state, so where does that leave rehabbers? They have to pay cash, which most don't want to do, or somehow get it renovated and then have it appraised for a mortgage. They're facing low rents, high turnover, and lots of headaches with such homes. When the typical landlord or flipper looks at a house and thinks, "Why would I want that albatross?" it's just the deal we're looking for.

As an aside, let me say that the market is so crazy, and as I write this, many such houses arc finding buyers. For the last decade, if you wanted to sell these properties, you had to do it with owner financing. No one was getting mortgages on them. Today, some people are. We are in an unusual stretch here, but I'm presenting strategies and scenarios that work regardless of temporary market conditions.

Landlords generally don't want these houses either, and yet, many of our buyers are investors who will act as landlords. That sounds like a contradiction, so let me explain.

Some of our buyers are people who might have poor credit or spotty employment histories but can swing a $4,000 down payment and $875 a month. They want to own a home to live in and improve, but they can't get a conventional mortgage. But as slow flippers, we also frequently sell to people in construction. They have the skills to rehab houses. Often, they have their own crews or own construction companies. These buyers, who I call "investors," have certain economies of scale. They can get the work done cheaply, and then keep the houses to operate as rentals without having to go to a bank or qualify for a mortgage. Their real business is construction, but the numbers on our deals work for them.

Why wouldn't such investors just get conventional mortgages? Well, many smaller contractors aren't great at keeping their paperwork, business licensing, and taxes in order. When you apply for a conventional mortgage, they want to see everything, including the kitchen sink—tax returns, bookkeeping, cash flow statements, profits, and losses.

Even many good small construction companies—people with plenty of jobs and cash—can't qualify for a pack of gum. This is why the slow flip exists. There are people out there who want houses but can't get them any other way.

At this point, some readers are thinking—probably in these exact terms—but I don't want to work in a warzone. I'm not going into the sort of dicey areas where you can find houses like this. People often think that the kinds of homes I'm describing only exist in really rough areas. In fact, they're much more widely available and in much better areas than you might guess. We buy what I call "the best of the worst." This means I don't buy in the worst, roughest spots. I don't buy any place I feel unsafe or uncomfortable. I do buy in what some would consider "bad areas," but only in the nicest parts of those areas—the best of the worst. You have to decide your own comfort level and the kinds of neighborhoods you want to work in. I have friends who buy in the toughest neighborhoods out there, and they do very well. I decided a long time ago that I didn't want to do that, though I am willing to buy in areas that might have seen better days. The distressed houses that we want for slow flips are available in many types of neighborhoods, though, not just "warzones."

How do we find these houses?

The Coming Boom

I'll present effective strategies for finding potential slow flips below, but first, I want to reiterate something I mentioned in the introduction: we are in the early stages of a golden age for slow flipping. I've been investing in real estate for decades, and I've never seen a better opportunity.

Why? To put it simply, landlords are tired, frustrated, and outraged after the COVID pandemic, and many of them want out. In a normal environment, when tenants don't pay, the landlord keeps their security deposits, starts eviction proceedings, and has them out of the unit in about six weeks. The process costs maybe $80, and a new tenant moves right in.

Then along came 2020 and a pandemic the likes of which we've never seen. The government said, "Sorry, no evictions. Your tenants aren't paying? Too bad, they don't have to." I don't want to go down a political rabbit hole here, but the important thing, for us as investors, is to consider the landlords' point of view. Rental housing is their product and livelihood, and suddenly, the government said, "Nope, you can't make the people who are using your product pay for it." The parallel, from a landlord's perspective, might be a supermarket in which people load up their carts and then at checkout, tell the cashier, "Sorry, I was affected by COVID, so I'm not paying."

Again, I'm not trying to make light of the economic hardships COVID caused for tenants, but imagine if you had to show up to work and do your job, but the government said certain clients using your services no longer had to pay you. You'd probably be frustrated and anxious. You'd have trouble paying the bills. You'd probably look for a new line of work eventually or call it quits and retire.

This is exactly what happened to landlords all over the country. Working for them means paying mortgages and insurance bills, making repairs, cutting lawns, meeting building codes, and performing endless other difficult chores. They had to keep doing all this work but in many cases, without being paid for it.

Many landlords who have been at it for decades are 65, 70, or 82 years old, and they've had it. They're angry about the money they lost, and some have wiped out their savings or are in debt. One landlord I've talked to about buying properties—he owns 84 or 85 of them—figured that he is owed $800,000 in lost rent from 2020. There was nothing he could do about it, and now, he wants to sell.

I have similar calls streaming in from people who have not one house or five, but 10, 20, or 50 houses they want to sell. I have one contract now on 16 houses sold as a package, and another landlord I'm talking to with 101 properties he wants to unload. Many landlords have evictions pending, and they're holding off on selling because the units will be worth more vacant than with non-paying tenants in residence, but a flood of these will be spilling into the market too.

The COVID chaos, which was so hard on landlords, creates an incredible opportunity for slow flipping. You don't need to feel bad about this since, as I've said, you are offering a valuable service. People want out; you're offering an exit.

To give you a sense of the growing opportunity for slow flipping, let me remind you that, as I said in the introduction, I have 138 properties, all slow flips, as I write this, in late 2022. That portfolio represents a lifetime's work of investing in real estate. In the next year, I believe that this number will double for me. Yes, I expect to make a lifetime's worth of investments in just one year. This is because I'll still buy single houses as they pop up. I'm now focusing on landlord packages with dozens of units for sale in one deal. If even a few of the larger packages work out, my portfolio will double.

As you wade into slow flipping, you'll realize that the general process is the same for larger deals and unconventional deals. We'll talk about some of those later in this chapter. Packages, or groups of rentals, do take more effort. If you pick up 30 rentals, you then have to turn them all into slow flips. That's hard work, but also rewarding and highly profitable.

Once you turn those deals into slow flips, you're insulated in a way that landlords are not. You're insulated from repairs, as we've discussed, and to a large degree, from market fluctuations and government edicts. Slow flippers were not burned by COVID the way landlords did because so many of our buyers are landlords themselves—investors or rehabbers, as well as individual homeowners. The landlords and many of our owner-occupant buyers too put new roofs on the properties, new siding, new windows, etc., and they're not going to walk away from those investments. Even if the tenants renting from our slow flip buyers stop paying, our buyers will usually bite the bullet and get us paid.

There has never in my lifetime been a better time to slow flip or more opportunity to build passive wealth and collect the checks that will help you realize your future vision. Keep that in mind as we explore some of the most effective strategies for finding slow flips below.

Other Investors

Our number one source for slow flips is other real estate investors. They do the same sort of marketing we do, using direct mail, signs, websites, Craigslist, and other methods, which we'll explore in this chapter. Housing wholesalers market in similar ways, as do rehabbers and landlords building their portfolios.

We're all casting wide nets as real estate investors, and we never know what they'll pull in. Other investors get deals they don't want for one reason or another, and some of those will be perfect for you. As I write this, I have four deals that came through from other investors in the last day, one of which I think I'm getting.

The last house I closed on also came through another investor. I won't go into the details, but it's what we call a "subject to," meaning I took over an existing mortgage. Another investor went on the appointment and contracted the property down to $40,000. He was happy to turn it over to me for $2,000, and I had to give the seller another $2,000, so for $4,000 out of pocket, I took over the house. My payments will be $675 a month, and I filled it the first weekend with a buyer paying $8,000 down and $1,175 a month.

For whatever reason, the deal didn't work for the other investor—a guy who does lots of houses—so he turned it over to me. I spent $4,000, and the next weekend, I got $8,000 back, and I'm now ahead $600 a month.

In this example, the house was large and in good shape, with an existing mortgage, so I did not have to use private money. That's not a typical deal, but you never know what other investors will turn up and turn over. Generally, we want to put the word out that we're open to buying the worst houses out there. Slow flippers are real estate's Statue of Liberty: *Give us your tired, your poor, your distressed houses ...* We're doing something most investors don't want to do, so they're happy to pass these deals on for a grand or several.

When I tell other investors about what we do in a slow flip, they say, "I would never do that, what a headache." But the truth is that these pricey big-box real estate seminars that fly into town, hold classes for three days, then fly out are essentially training people to buy our houses. Like many of the popular books and online programs, they tell people to look for properties with low money down, so that they can cash hundreds of dollars a month.

The people attending those seminars often wind up buying our properties once we've arranged owner-financing, so selling these isn't an issue, but we're buying them when no one else wants to.

The house pictured below, in the before and after photos, is a prime example. The entire marketplace saw this deal, mocked it, laughed, and said, "No way, I would never buy that." Another investor posted it to a local investor group I'm a part of, so I got the email and watched the mockery.

I watched and watched ... Eventually, I said, "Hey, is that house still available?" It was. I met this investor at the house and within minutes, said, "I'll take it." I paid about $18,000 for it. I only had to borrow the purchase price, so my payment was something like $380 a month. I sold to an investor-buyer who did a beautiful job rehabbing the house. He took great pride in his work. I like to show this one because I was able to take good before and after pics and videos of the property and interview the buyer while he was still in the house.

This house turned out to be a fantastic deal, and I've had a lot of great deals come to me through other investors. How do you get in touch with them? Start with local real estate investment associations, clubs, and meet-ups. In many areas, a simple Google search will give you some contacts and ideas. Sign up for email lists, join local investor clubs, get into online groups, and attend local meetings. Facebook Marketplace and Craigslist, which we'll cover next, can also lead to meeting other investors and finding out about clubs and groups in your area.

As you build your contact list of other investors, let them know that your criteria are different from most investors'. Your constant refrain should be, "I want you to send me your worst." Get that word out there, and other investors will realize you're not in competition with them.

They will start to see you as a great outlet for deals they don't want to do but can make a finder's fee on or for houses they want to unload. In turn, you might send tips about houses that are perfect for rehabbing but out of your price range, or just not for you, to other investors, building good will.

Craigslist & Facebook Marketplace

Craigslist and Facebook Marketplace are both huge sources of leads for slow-flip houses. On Craigslist, simply click on "housing" and then "real estate for sale." Type in your location, and bingo, you're ready to start browsing for houses. On Facebook, click on "Marketplace" on the left-hand side of your home screen, scroll down through "Categories," and click on "Home Sales."

Checking these sites doesn't take long, and I recommend that you do it every day. It's a great way to get a feel for your target market, whether that's the town you live in or another with more affordable pricing. Anyone skeptical about houses in our price range existing out there will be surprised. You'll start seeing them as you browse these sites. Try it today! Deals are there, waiting for you.

On sites like Craigslist and Facebook Marketplace, the best houses go quickly, often in minutes. The distressed or "ugly" houses we want to slow flip will sit and sit, listed at $20,000, $30,000, or $40,000. Most investors don't want them, and the buyers who might be interested can't qualify for conventional mortgages and don't have the cash for an outright purchase.

When you pick up these houses and then put them back on Facebook Marketplace or Craigslist for sale, however, they will go quickly—the exact same houses. Again, this is because we're really selling the financing. The house that dozens of buyers passed over because they can't get a bank loan and don't have $30,000 in cash to buy outright is now accessible for $3,000 down and $875 a month. Buyers who would have passed a house over last week can now consider it because you're making a purchase possible, creating an opportunity with owner financing and no credit check.

Facebook Wholesaling Groups

The internet has made slow flipping easier in countless ways. Wholesaling networks have been around forever, but finding and joining them used to take more effort. Today, you can simply type "house wholesaling groups" into the search bar on Facebook, and a bunch will pop up. Type in your area too. Kokomo, IN; Buffalo, NY, or wherever. If you live in a city like Seattle or a state like California where slow flip deals will be difficult or impossible to find, you can type in the target market where you think you might do deals (it's easy to do slow flips long-distance, and we'll get to the logistics of that later).

I've mentioned "wholesaling" without explaining the process because it's not our focus here. Basically, wholesalers contract a property, mark up the price, and sell it to another investor, who will rehab and retail it himself. Wholesalers do not provide owner-financing. They find a deal, agree to a price, and sign a contract that's "assignable." Before the closing date, the wholesaler assigns that contract to an investor-buyer who pays them an "assignment fee" and is then bound by the original price and terms.

I hope that you can already see how finding wholesalers with deals that work for you can be a great source of slow flips. The wholesaler has done the looking and negotiating for you, saving you time and hassle. On your end, you simply have to look at the numbers and make sure the house will work as a slow flip at the wholesaler's price. If so, you take over the contract, purchase the house with private money, and then market it to potential buyers with owner-financing. The wholesaler flips the contract, and you slow flip the house.

I am a member of many wholesaling groups on Facebook, including a number outside the state of Virginia, where I live. I don't do slow flips in all of the states I monitor. I am interested in some and might eventually buy into them, but I also have students from all over, and I watch various markets for them. I'm also in wholesaling groups in Hampton Roads, Virginia Beach, Norfolk, and other markets close to home.

I am in a bunch of wholesaling groups in St. Louis because I've considered investing there. I will take my time before plunging into a new market, though, because I have an infrastructure to set up. I don't have employees, but in Virginia, I have people who put up my signs, attend court hearings for me, process evictions, etc. If I go into a new market, I want to pick one new place and go in heavy, to make that infrastructure worthwhile. I don't want to plunge into someplace new just to buy three properties.

That infrastructure, which thanks to technology, is easier than ever to utilize and is part of why slow flipping at a distance is doable. I work with people who live in other states and invest in my area, and I know people in my area investing in other states. I have a guy we've talked to about deals who lives in Israel. He has about a dozen slow flips and 20 rentals that he bought as a package. He did those deals not just long-distance, but from another country.

You can absolutely slow flip at a distance, so don't let the notion that you live in California, Brooklyn, or Boston, where prices are too high, discourage you. We'll talk more about the logistics later, but remember that when you slow flip, you are essentially a finance company. I can't emphasize this enough. Do not think of yourself as a landlord or get attached to the properties you're buying.

In fact, do not even think of yourself as being "in real estate." You are in finance. You are doing simple math—*how much can we buy for, sell for, and collect monthly?* That's your job. Yes, you own the property, but you're just shuffling papers. As soon as you own the house, you're selling it, that day or the next. It exists for you primarily on paper, and the real product that makes you appealing to potential buyers is financing, not real estate.

The Multiple Listing Service (MLS)

The MLS, or Multiple Listing Service, as many readers know, is a private database in a particular locality used by real estate agents to share information. MLS access previously gave you the keys to the kingdom. It was the way that realtors made money because only they had access to details about everything bought, sold, and on market. That's much less true in an era when websites like Zillow, Trulia, and Redfin provide rich public info, but sometimes, things pop up or change on the MLS and not in other places online.

The MLS can give you an inside track. If a property is in the MLS, it means there's an agent involved, and with slow flips, we usually steer clear of agent-marketed properties. They're generally too expensive to make our deals work, but sometimes, an owner who needs a quick sale hires an agent, and the house is listed at a ridiculously low price. Agents also deal with bank-owned foreclosed properties, which often sell for a song.

The demand for the properties we want isn't high, so you can sometimes spot deals in the MLS, depending on the market. In some places, you can find an abundance of deals through the MLS. I still peruse the MLS in my area, but I haven't been very successful with buying slow flips there, in Virginia. Deals do emerge, and somebody gets them, so it's worth following. Even if the listings aren't within our parameters, I'll make low offers. If one responds, great. If not, no sweat. We get what we get.

Because the MLS is a private database, you generally need to be a licensed real estate agent to gain access. If you have your license, you're in business. If not, you can cultivate a relationship with an agent or agents who can give you access. Let them know that you plan on buying and selling properties, and they'll see the potential mutual benefit. If they tip you off on distressed houses that turn into slow flips for you, you can pay them a finder's fee, and you might very well come across houses out of your range that turns into listings for them. Fortunately, with sites like Zillow and Redfin, most of what's on the MLS today is accessible to anyone as a buyer free of charge online.

Deal Machine

Deal Machine is an incredible app you can download on your phone. It has become popular with wholesalers and real estate investors generally, and it's a powerful way to find slow flips. The app keeps growing and adding utility, but it's best known for its "driving-for-dollars" feature. Driving for dollars is an old tried-and-true method for finding deals that work just as you would imagine based on that name. You get in the car and start cruising neighborhood streets, scouting for houses that look distressed, vacant, uncared-for, etc.

In the old days, you would jot down an address and any other info you might glean from perusing a house, and then attempt to track down an owner, contact info, and details about the property, using public records, reverse directories, etc. Sounds arduous? Yup, it was.

Enter Deal Machine. It is not in every market, but in the places where it's available, the app locks on your location and gives you a map on the screen. Tap on the properties on your phone that you're driving past, and info about the house and owner will pop up. Is the property vacant? Is there an absentee owner? What's the equity situation? It's all there at your fingertips.

From the info provided, you can create your own lists of leads, then can contact them using the Deal Machine database to get emails, phone numbers, addresses, etc. You can reach out yourself with a call, email, or send a direct mail piece right through the app. Yes, the app will handle automated postcards and send them to potential, motivated sellers for you.

The app also helps you to manage follow-up, which is critical, to staying on top of the leads you've assembled. A list-builder option allows you to filter for categories like vacant, foreclosure, pre-foreclosure, bank-owned, absentee, etc. I love Deal Machine. We do a lot of deals through it, and I highly recommend it to everyone.

If you would like to try Deal Machine, I have a coupon code for a free trial: use code FREE15 to get a two-week free trial.

Smart Direct Mail

There's a reason your mailbox is always full of direct-mail marketing from restaurants, realtors, hospitals, shoe stores, and so on. Direct mail works. Those who predicted that social media and online marketing would spell the end of direct mail were simply wrong. Your ROI, or Return on Investment, with direct mail is high, especially if you're smart about it.

I like direct mail partly because letters and postcards that come directly into your mailbox can feel personal, and that gets you attention in a world where it's in short supply. Even more important, direct mail allows for sharp targeting, so you only go after the people you want. The smarter your targeting, the better your ROI.

You can pick the price point you're going after—houses valued at $80,000 or under $100,000, or in other ranges. You can target using equity—I only want to mail people who own their houses free and clear, for example. You can aim for absentee owners, owners of vacant properties, out-of-state absentee owners, etc. You choose your criteria and get your piece mailed to the selected audience.

Many books have been written about effective direct-mail marketing. That's not our focus, so I won't devote more space to it here, but I will print a QR code below for a company that we use called REI Print Mail. I love this firm because it will shock no one to learn that I am not the most tech-savvy guy. I can sit in front of the computer trying to get a mailing set up for longer than I care to admit, and inevitably, I'll get frustrated. I wind up saying, "Forget it, I'll do it another time," which means I get behind in a business where delays equal lost deals.

REI Print Mail will assign you a direct-mail coach, and they can walk you through the whole process over the phone. Simply tell them your targets, price points, areas, etc., and they'll send you a proof to tell you how many people meet those criteria. You hit "Approve," and they do the rest. If you are tech-savvy and don't need a coach, you can forego that option, do your own legwork, and they'll just print and mail whatever you order.

There is a lot to learn upfront on slow flipping, and one of the keys is to keep things as simple and efficient as you can. I am a big fan of systems. I automate and delegate whenever possible, and that's been a big part of my success. Mailing postcards and letters is a piece of the puzzle I'm happy to have someone else handle once I spell out what I want.

Bandit Signs

I don't particularly like bandit signs, but they work. These are the small, corrugated plastic signs that you see on the side of the road. People call them bandit signs because, well, strictly speaking, they're not exactly legal in most areas. Advertisers must put them out at night or in the early morning to avoid problems. I know of just one person who actually was arrested for erecting bandit signs. Usually, the authorities simply take them away or call with a warning. Apart from the legal issue, I resist bandit signs because so many people use them for so many businesses. They can turn a street into a cluttered mess. I hated hanging these signs so much, that when I started using them, I hired a guy to install and remove them for me.

If you decide to use bandit signs, my advice is to keep it simple: WE BUY HOUSES and your phone number. I always make mine yellow and black, 18 x 24 inches, basic but professionally printed. That works. When you try to explain your business or include a Web address, it's too much for passing drivers to read. I am opposed to handwritten signs when you're looking for houses to buy. They'll just get you laughed at (I have a very different philosophy when it comes to your house-for-sale signs, which we'll get to in the next chapter).

Your Existing Rentals

Another less-than-obvious source of slow flips as you look to build long-term passive wealth might be your existing rentals. Some readers, I'm sure, are interested in the slow flip because they already have rentals, and managing them is more of a headache than they could have imagined. People sometimes tell me that they would like to get into slow flipping, but they already have 10 rentals or however many, and that's all they can handle.

Converting your own rentals to slow flips is always an option. This strategy allows you to build passive wealth while eliminating the stress and headaches that come with being a landlord. How does it work? Well, think about the slow flip. As we know by now, it has two parts:

1. Finance a distressed house with private money in a way that lets you pay it off in five years.
2. Sell the house at retail with owner financing in a way that lets a buyer pay you off over 30 years.

We've been talking about the process in terms of both parts, but you can do the second part of the process without part 1. There's no reason that you can't take an existing rental and sell it on a 30-year mortgage with owner financing. Why would you convert an existing rental to a slow flip? Let's look at a practical example.

Say you own a $200,000 house and you collect $1,800 a month in rent for it, and that's the highest the market will bear. You have a mortgage on this house, with a monthly payment of $1,200. That leaves you with $600 a month, but from that amount, you must pay taxes and insurance as well as maintenance and repairs. You probably don't have much afterward, not to mention the fact that you're getting complaints about the water pressure, a broken AC unit, a perennially clogged toilet, etc. every week.

You can offer the house for sale to your existing tenants or wait until their lease is up and sell it to a new buyer-investor with owner financing. I would probably market the $200,000 house for sale with a down payment of $15,000 to $25,000 and a monthly payment of about $1,800, or a little more.

The monthly payment you collect will remain the same, but you're no longer responsible when a faucet leaks or the furnace quits. You don't have to shovel snow or mow the lawn. When the buyer calls you to complain about a pipe leaking, you say, "Okay, call a plumber." I always reply to these calls this way, *"You wouldn't call Bank of America and tell them you have a leaky sink, would you?" "Well, don't call me either." "I'm your finance company, not your landlord."*

Okay, you eliminate headaches, but you're giving away your equity in your house over 30 years, right? That's one way to look at it, but as we've discussed, your buyer is unlikely to stay in the property. There's a good chance they'll give it back to you in two, three, or seven years, at which point, they won't have built up much equity. If the house returns to you, you find a new buyer, collect a new down payment, and restart the clock.

Also, remember how amortization works, as we explored earlier. If the buyer puts down $20,000 and you finance the remaining $180,000 on the house with a monthly payment of $1,824, the interest rate will be around 11.8 percent. This means that the total cost of the loan is

$656,582, not $200,000. The interest paid will come to $476,582. That's significantly more than double the value of the house today, and the buyer will pay mostly interest, building almost no equity over the next decade.

Rental conversion to a slow flip

House Value	$200,000
Down Payment	$20,000
Loan Amount	$180,000
Loan Term	30 Years
Monthly Payment	$1,824
Interest Rate	11.8%
Total Interest	$476,582
Total Loan Cost	$656,582

When I buy properties as a package, they typically are rentals, with tenants living in them. We immediately send a letter stating that we purchased the property at 123 Main Street, and since we do not operate rentals, we won't be renewing their leases. However, if they are interested, we would be willing to finance their purchase of the house. Because they're already in the property, we write, and we will not charge a down payment if they're interested. The new payment on their mortgage would be X amount per month over 30 years.

I usually try to make the mortgage payment slightly higher than the monthly rent and make it an odd number. I do this because odd numbers look more like mortgage payments while even numbers look like rent. It is a mortgage payment—there's no scam here—but because you're dealing with someone who has been renting the property, I want to drive home the idea that they'll be buyers now, with all of the attached responsibilities, and no longer tenants.

If you're interested, our letter concludes, call and we'll set up a time to do the paperwork. The current tenants take this offer almost 100 percent of the time. Usually, they're thrilled at the opportunity. They have wanted to buy but just didn't have the ability.

About now, some readers might be thinking that this is taking advantage of people or making them pay more than a place is worth. Apart from the ethics of such a move, won't the buyer figure this out eventually and be outraged?

The opposite is true. You'll have people hugging you, thanking you, and crying about how you saved their lives. They've wanted to buy for so long and finally...

It's easy for you to think, "I'm making so much money. I must be doing something wrong." Right?

No! Look at it from the buyer's perspective. They are paying roughly the same amount each month that they would have paid in rent. If they managed to buy somewhere else (many can't, by the way, or they already would have), they would pay a mortgage company. Instead, they're paying you, but they didn't have to jump through the hoops of qualifying—turning over tax returns, explaining spotty employment, and supplying banking and cash flow statements.

If there is a buyer who wants to rent out the unit to someone else—often the case—now, they're able to start building a portfolio. With one house under their belt, they might soon have two, three, or five. I have people who bought a couple of slow flips from me but probably have 10 rental houses total if we add up the ones they bought from my group and coaching students.

I have one buyer who works as a cop in Norfolk by day. He has three houses from me, bought with owner financing on the model I've presented here, and others bought from people in my group. He rents out rooms by the week in those houses, and he's crushing it. He pays us around $1,100 a month for one house I bought for $15,000, but he's getting $2,800 to $2,900 a month in rent.

This buyer received a valuable service from me, as your buyers will from you. Don't think you're taking advantage of anyone. It's okay to buy something for $30,000 and sell it for $90,000. It's okay to collect payments that early on, go mostly to interest, not principal—that's how every bank does it. You're providing value and selling financing. The house is just part of the package.

Unconventional Slow Flips

So far, I've promoted a tidy model for slow flips—a distressed house selling for $30,000, with owner financing over 30 years at 12 percent interest. These parameters work, and I want you to keep them front and center as you start investing. I also want you to realize that other scenarios that don't match our criteria will arise and might make for great slow flips. The template is solid, but you can modify it to fit your needs or the contours of a good opportunity.

In this section, I'll give you a few examples of unconventional slow flips that were found outside the standard box but became phenomenal deals nonetheless. Once you understand the slow flip, you can apply the formula to just about anything in real estate.

- **Mason Lodge.** My first example is Mason Lodge, a former Masonic lodge. This is the 8,000-square-foot commercial building I mentioned in Chapter 2. I don't normally buy commercial properties, but using a creative slow flip strategy, I basically got this one for free, and it turned into one of my best deals.

A guy called me about the property, a big brick building on a sizeable site. I wasn't really interested, but he told me I could get it for $195,000. The city assessment had it valued at $495,000, so I thought, "Okay, I guess I'll figure out something to do with this." I contracted the property and tried to wholesale it (remember, that means flipping the contract to someone else who pays me an "assignment fee" and then closes on it). I figured that a buyer could bulldoze the building and build seven houses on the site. That seemed worthy of an assignment fee of around $100,000.

I didn't have any luck, well, not much. I got offers. I could have taken a $50,000 assignment fee on it but decided not to. That would have been half what I'd aimed for, and it just didn't seem worth selling at that price. I preferred to keep it, so I closed on the property, using my own money. Building new housing on-site still seemed like a good idea, given the size of the parcel, and looking at the layout, I thought, "We can break off three lots and leave the old building intact." We separated three lots from the main property where someone could construct new homes, and I sold them for $60,000 each.

If you're following the numbers, I paid $195,000 for the property, and by selling off a piece of it, I quickly got back $180,000 of my purchase price (3 lots x $60,000 each), leaving me just $15,000 out of pocket. I then sold the building on a slow flip for $499,000, with owner financing. This deal was much bigger than the typical slow flip but worked the same way. The woman who bought the property gave me a $25,000 down payment and agreed to monthly payments of $4,977.

Remember, I was only $15,000 out of pocket before my buyer looked at the building. Once she took it and handed me $25,000, I was free and clear. The $180,000 I got from selling the three lots plus her $25,000 paid off my original investment, with $10,000 left over. I received all my money back and then some, and now I collect $60,000 a year from her—roughly $5,000 a month x 12— in pure profit. I have no mortgage, no private money to pay back, no debt, and $5,000 a month in income that, ultimately, cost me nothing.

Purchase Price	$195,000
3 Lots sold	$180,000
Buyer's Down Payment	$25,000
Building Sale	$499,000
Monthly Payment / Cash flow	$4,977

- **Family house.** Needless to say, I love the Mason Lodge deal, though it doesn't fit into the typical slow flip box. Neither did the last personal house I sold, the one my family and I lived in before our current house. This second example wound up selling with a conventional mortgage, but I first tried to structure it as a slow flip, and that led to a better deal in the end.

I owned this family house free and clear when we decided to sell. It was worth about $600,000, but the highest sale price in the area at the time was $570,000. We were going to list it with an agent, who wanted to put it on the market at $570,000. I did the math and figured I would walk away with about $500,000 after paying for agent commissions, closing-cost assistance, the repairs buyers would want post-inspection, etc.

If I'm going to walk away with $500,000 in a conventional sale, I figured, I can get a new mortgage on the property at a ridiculously low rate and pull out that same $500,000, but from a lender. I would still have about $100,000 in equity in the property since the mortgage wouldn't be for the full value, and I could sell it as a slow flip to create an income stream that would cover my mortgage until it was paid off.

With that plan in mind, I marketed the house on Facebook Marketplace to find a buyer for $600,000, even though, as I said, $570,000 was the highest number in the area. I structured the deal so that a buyer could put $5,000 down and have a monthly payment of $4,200. My payment to the bank was going to be around $2,200, so I'd be retaining a good cash flow property.

The very first people who came out to see the house loved it. They said they wanted to buy it but preferred to get their own mortgage if that was okay with me. That suited me just fine. I said, "As long as you're paying this price and agree that it's not contingent on appraisal, we're good (the lack of comparable properties and that $570,000 ceiling could have created appraisal problems)." "Also, I'm not paying any agent commissions or closing cost assistance, and I'm not doing repairs." They agreed, and the house closed at $600,000.

So instead of taking $500,000, my check at closing was $596,000. Even though the deal ultimately did not turn into a slow flip (they used a conventional lender, not me, for financing), starting out that way saved me a fortune. In slow flip fashion, the house was sold "as is," with no repairs, agent commissions, closing-cost assistance, etc.

- **The package of eight.** This was another of my best deals ever, resulting in nearly $1 million in equity and $5,000 a month cash flow, with nothing out of pocket for me. Buying a group of properties—in this case, eight rentals—often means altering the slow flip formula and sometimes changing it in ways that benefit your bottom line.

I worked on this deal for about a year, but the landlord who was thinking of selling these eight rentals as a group decided he wanted to keep them. In March 2021, he called to ask if my offer was still good. We had lunch to talk it over. I'd made him the kind of three-way offer I'm sure some readers are familiar with—a cash offer, a financing offer, and another owner-financing offer. It seemed like he wanted to go for the owner-financing offer, which meant that he would finance my purchase over 10 years, with an interest rate of around 4 percent and a $50,000 down payment from me.

At lunch, he brought up the owner-financing deal, and at a moment, I'll never forget; I said, "We like this offer, but would you mind not putting any money down? We'd really rather have that in the monthly payments." I was biting my lip, trying to contain my excitement, but after a moment, he said, "Hmm, yes, I think I could do that."

I got the properties—eight nice places in Norfolk—for about $64,000 each, with no money down. If only every deal could be like this one! I had financing for 10 years, with zero dollars out of pocket. I immediately sold them all as slow flips. At six of the eight houses, I converted the existing tenants into buyers, along the same lines we discussed in the last section, and I found new buyers for the other two. The sales price was $179,000 each, with owner financing and payments of $1,175 a month from my buyers over 30 years.

In total, I made around $1 million in equity on this one transaction and created $5,000 a month in positive cash flow, without having to put a penny down. In 10 years, when my 10-year mortgage with the seller is up, the cash flow will double to $10,000 a month.

Package of 8 Slow Flip	Per Unit	Total for 8
Purchase Price	$64,000	$512,000
Down Payment	$0	$0
My Mortgage Payment	$550	$4,400
Sales Price	$179,000	$1.432 million
Buyers' Payments	$1,175	$9,400
Monthly Cash flow	$625	$5,000

- **The package of six.** This was a six-unit rental property that a student of mine slow-flipped in a great deal, though it didn't fit the standard template. He found the rundown six-plex and skip traced the owner ("skip tracing" is the process of tracking down someone difficult to find—as in, they might have "skipped" town—and it's easier than ever, thanks to the internet, as you'll see if you googled the term).

My student called the owner directly, and he agreed to finance the sale. From his perspective, the rentals had become a burden, and the idea of an exit looked attractive. Taking this sale on an unappealing property would provide him with a steady monthly cash flow minus all the headaches that come with being the landlord for units that have seen better days.

The price that the buyer and seller agreed on was $175,000. My student put about $17,000 down and the owner agreed to finance the rest over 21 years, collecting a monthly payment of about $1,200.

We turned around and sold the whole package immediately as one slow flip. My student never collected a single month's rent and never fielded a single tenant complaint, which is the whole point of doing a slow flip instead of rentals. The six-unit package sold for $299,000, with $25,000 down and owner financing—this time, provided by my student—over 30 years. That meant he would collect a monthly payment of $2,900.

Think about the math here. My student, who put $17,000 down to buy the place, got all his money back right off the bat with that $25,000 down payment, and he began receiving a monthly payment of $2,900. Now, out of that $2,900, he had to pay his seller, as well as taxes and insurance, but that left him ahead by about $1,200 a month. He has no money invested in this property and he's ahead by $1,200 a month for the first 21 years. At that point, when his mortgage is paid, the monthly payment he keeps jumps to $3,000 a month.

I believe this was my student's third slow flip, a deal he found and cultivated and obviously, loves. You don't need too many deals like this to change your life. The point, again, is that while this one is a slow flip, it doesn't fit our standard formula. The purchase and sales prices are much higher than usual. We're dealing with owner-financing on the purchase as well as the sale, and the term for our mortgage is 21 years, not five. It all works in this case because after you run the numbers, you're still $1,200 ahead for the next 21 years, whereas in our typical slow flip, you break even until you pay back your private-money lender. We usually suffer for five years to get to freedom faster, but in this unconventional deal, there's no suffering—just cash flow and then better cash flow.

Note that in the chart below, we leave our buyers' cash flow blank. If they renovate the property, raise rents, and operate efficiently, they could have substantial cash flow. If they struggle month to month like many landlords, they'll be lucky to make a couple of hundred bucks or break even after mortgage payments, maintenance, repairs, vacancies, etc. Not to sound callous, but those are the buyers' problems, not ours, and they're likely the same ones that caused the original landlord to let the property slide and then sell it to us. We avoid all such headaches with the slow flip, operating like Mr. Burns and dealing in paper, not leaky faucets or light bulbs.

The six-plex slow flip	For My Student	For His Buyer
Sale Price	$175,00	$299,000
Down Payment	$17,000	$25,000
Interest Rate	8%	12%
Term	21 Years	30 Years
Payment, 1st 21 Years	$1,200	$2,900
Payment, Last 9 Years	$0	$2,900
Cash flow, 1st 21 Years	$1,200	?
Cash flow, Last 9 Years	$3,000	?

I could supply many more examples of unconventional slow flips, deals done by me, as well as by my students, over the years. They would all have different parameters, some varying slightly from our standard formula, with a higher price tag, lower interest, or varied terms. Some, like the examples above, would be quite different from our template— multi-unit properties, commercial properties, no private money, no money down ...

As you get your feet wet slow flipping, you'll see that the structure of a slow flip can be used creatively in just about any real estate context.

I've been at this for a long time, and I'm still discovering new ways to use the same basic model.

Closing as a Buyer

Once you've found a slow-flip property to purchase, the closing is simple—basically, the same process you have used if you ever bought a house. You sign a purchase agreement with the seller and get it to your attorney. If you're using private money, the attorney will draw up a note and deed of trust. This document spells out the terms of the loan and your promise to pay it back, and it allows the private-money lender to take control of the property if you fail to pay back your loan. This is essentially the same kind of mechanism used when banks issue mortgages.

The attorney will then run a title search to make sure that ownership of the property is clear and determine if there are any claims against it. In some states, you might deal directly with a title company to get the title search done. Liens against the property are not unusual and don't typically wreck a deal. If the seller owes $4,000 to a contractor or $11,000 to a hospital, those amounts will come out of the proceeds at closing and be paid off. You will purchase title insurance—again, from the title company—which protects you and your lender from any claims that might arise later from, say, faulty documents, conflicting wills, missed liens, tax bills, etc.

Your attorney or someone from the title company will sit in at closing and sign with you. If you buy the house for $30,000 and there's a lien from St. John's Hospital for $10,000, the lawyer will take $10,000 from the proceeds and pay off the hospital. The seller will collect $20,000 or whatever remains after the debt is paid. Liens aren't an issue unless they add up to more than the amount of the sale. In that case, the liens, or at least some of them, would have to be taken care of before the sale could go through.

As the buyer, you pay closing costs when you purchase a slow flip, but they don't amount to much. The lawyer fee might be $350, the title search for $200, and transfer taxes (several hundred—these vary, depending on the sate). All told, my closing costs on a typical slow flip in Virginia are $800 to $1,000. In Chapter 5, we'll talk about closing your slow flips as a seller—an even simpler process that works a little differently.

You now have a grasp of the slow flip formula and a good start on the best ways to find and buy potential slow flips. In Chapter 4, we'll explore the second half of the slow flip process—finding buyers and investors to fill your houses and your main job (cashing checks).

4

Marketing Slow Flips

As you begin slow flipping, you'll see that marketing is a huge part of the business. Marketing yourself and your ability to buy distressed houses—offering a quick, painless exit for homeowners—is key to finding slow flips, as we saw in Chapter 3. Marketing your financing package and the houses you've purchased is key to filling slow flips, as we'll see in this chapter.

You need to have a solid marketing strategy in place before a good slow flip comes along so that you can sell it as soon as you close. As I've said, you want to do this without any renovations or, ideally, even cleanup. In this chapter, we'll explore a variety of strategies for filling slow flips quickly. It's important to get buyers into houses without delay. You always want to be covering your own mortgage payments for the first five years of a slow flip and making a profit after you're paid up, starting with that magical 61st month when you own it free and clear. A vacant property doesn't make money, and having a good marketing infrastructure in place makes keeping slow flips occupied fast and simple.

New investors are often unduly nervous about this part of the process. What if I can't find buyers? With a little know-how, finding buyers has always been the easy part. Remember, you're offering homeownership for $3,000 to $5,000 down and a monthly payment of $875, with no credit or employment check. This sort of opportunity is extremely attractive to a huge number of people in any market. And thanks to technology, websites, and apps like Facebook Marketplace, Craigslist, and MyDealFactory.com, marketing slow flips has gotten even easier. In this chapter, I'll walk you through the simple steps to finding buyers both online and with effective low-tech strategies, including ridiculous, misspelled signs (Don't laugh! They work incredibly well, as you'll soon see).

Don't Ask, Don't Tell

We'll talk about a variety of marketing tools in this chapter, but before we get to them, I want to give you a bedrock principle that applies across the board. This tip regarding the price you advertise and give to potential buyers is worth the cost of this book 100 times over. It's so helpful and common sense. I'm amazed that the world does not live by it. Here it is, eliminate the word "asking" from your vocabulary. It pains and kills me when I see people advertising anything, not just houses—could be cars, a watch, a computer, whatever—by stating that they're "asking" $5,000, $300, or $975 a month. All "asking" means is that you'll take less. The price is negotiable, and when we slow flip, we're not negotiable. The price is the price. You're selling for $3,000 down, $875 a month. You're selling for $5,000 down, $1,175 a month. End of story. You've done the math; these are the numbers that work for you, and they constitute a great deal for some buyers.

You're not "asking" anything because you don't want to haggle. Your formula doesn't allow for it. You don't want to waste your time on it, and when you're firm, you don't need to negotiate. If a buyer doesn't like your terms, they can move on. That one simple word, the A-word (it pains me too much to type it out again!) is an invitation to haggle. No, it's more a guarantee of haggling, and if you've used the A-word, the ensuing negotiations won't be the buyer's fault. If you wanted a good used car and found one "for sale" with a sign that said "Asking $5,000." Would you simply write a check for $5,000? No! Everyone reading this right now would say, "How about $4,000? Would you take $3,500? What's the lowest you can go?" "Asking" means I'll take less, so you'd be a fool not to try for a lower price. You might as well write "hoping." Asking $5,000 is essentially the same as saying that you're "hoping for $5,000."

There will be deals when you can go lower on price and still make them work, but even then, you don't want to start by announcing wiggle room. "Asking" equals flexibility, and you don't want to appear flexible. You want to run a business and have a set of rules for it. So, no more "asking"—not on signs or websites, not in texts, Facebook ads, Craigslist ads, etc.

Horrible Signs

We might as well start our discussion of marketing tools with a low-tech one—the ridiculous signs I mentioned earlier. They're a tried-and-true method, requiring zero know-how, beyond the ability to write. I won't add "spell" because poor spelling might actually help you, as I discovered by accident. Here's the story.

When I'm out and about, I always have blank signs in the back of my car. I don't usually write them out myself because my handwriting is deplorable. One day, in 2008, however, I went to a house by myself. A tenant had left, and as it turns out, he hid the key. I was locked out of my own house, which I wanted to fill with a new buyer ASAP. Well, I thought, I'm here anyway. I might as well put some for-sale signs out. I handwrote them and stuck them in front of the house, as well as around the neighborhood.

Almost immediately, my phone was ringing like crazy, literally within an hour of leaving the property. Off the hook! By the next day—24 hours later—I had somebody for the house. I went back, picked up the signs, and dropped them at my office.

I didn't think anything of it—one of those lucky days—and then, a couple of weeks later, a guy who did some work for me came in and said, "What's a chep house?"

"Excuse me?" I said.

"Behind you," he said, pointing. "The sign for a C-H-E-P house. What is that?"

I was so embarrassed. I would have invented some sort of financing program on the spot if I could have thought of something CHEP might stand for County Housing Economical ... Instead, I had to admit that the sign should have read "CHEAP," as in very affordable, "HOUSE."

I had no idea I'd misspelled the word. Horrible, right? Or was it?

I started to wonder if the poor spelling was why my phone went crazy. Intrigued, I started running tests. Everything I do is a test—every ad, sign, or call—because I'm constantly trying to see what works best. I started recording results from my nice signs and from a batch of crappy signs. The results weren't even close. The crappy signs beat the nice ones with a response rate of 20:1 respectively. Not only that, the crappier the signs were, the more responses I got. The more I misspelled words or squeezed them in or put things out of sequence, the better the response.

Of course, I followed up with the people who responded as we did the paperwork and found out why. Suppose you have bad credit or a spotty employment history or you're an investor with no credit, or you simply don't have much money on hand. Whatever the situation, you're the kind of person banks don't want to darken their doorways. You see a beautiful RE/MAX sign, a sign for a slick real estate agent pictured with perfect hair, or a marketing piece that looks permanent. It's so well printed.

What's your response?

"These guys are going to want a $45 application fee, and I'm going to get denied anyway! I've been down this road before. No way, why even mess with it?"

But when that same person with a low bank balance or poor credit sees a horrible handwritten sign with spelling errors and cramped letters, they think, *"Here's someone I can deal with. They probably don't even realize they could get more for this house if they cleaned it up. I might have a chance with this person…"*

Such buyers do have a chance, and that's why your phone rings off the hook. I've lived this experiment firsthand, but don't take my word for it. Try it yourself. It's difficult for some people to do, I know. We feel foolish misspelling words or writing like a third-grader, but it works. Make your own horrible signs, or if you have a local person on the ground putting out signs for you, tell them exactly what you want—rough, scruffy, *un*professional, misspelled, CHEP HOUSE! The response will be 20-to-1 over neat, professional signage. If you want a sign you can be proud of, get it professionally made. If you want a sign that fills houses, do it my way.

I should remind readers here that this strategy only works for selling houses and filling your slow flips. You don't want to do this with the "bandit" signs we use to find slow flips. Those signs, as I mentioned earlier, should be simple and professional. Mine are yellow and black, 18 x 24 inches, made by a printer. The idea that you're not sophisticated appeals to buyers, who think, this is someone simple who really needs to sell this house *"They don't know enough to take advantage of me."* Sellers, though, are wary of someone who promises to buy their house but might lack the ability to follow through. *"They don't know enough to make a sign, can they handle a sale?"*

Ghost Signs

While we're on the subject of signs, I should say that they can be a great way not just to fill your slow flips, but also to test the waters—for a specific property or the market generally—and to build your buyers' list.

Let's say, you're working on buying a house. You don't own it yet, but you're talking with the sellers. They're interested, and you're interested, but you're also concerned. You're thinking to yourself, "How do I know if people will want this? How do I know if I can find a buyer?" This is a common worry when you're starting. You can build your confidence and get a head start on marketing by putting out signs before you buy the house. Obviously, you can't put a for-sale sign in front of the house since you don't own it, but you can stick a number of them around the neighborhood, advertising the same basic info, obviously, without a specific address.

Cheap House

$89,000

$4,000 Down

Owner Will Finance

No Credit Check

CALL 555-0000

If you're working a long-distance market, you can pay someone to put up these signs, or not, but it's easy to do yourself if you're local. Make some horrible-looking signs like the one in the photo below—one I actually used recently—and post them in the vicinity of the house you're interested in.

As calls come in, you can judge the response and gauge the local market for what you hope you will soon be selling. How many people are, in fact, interested in a house like this, with $3,000 or $5,000 down and owner financing?

You get a feel for the demand, and here's the important part, you build a buyers' list. Take down the information of everyone who calls. When someone says, "Hey, I was calling about that sign advertising a house for sale," you'd reply, "Well, I haven't closed on it yet. Let me get your information, and as soon as I close, you'll be the first one I call to come to take a look at it."

This works, by the way, even if you don't have a specific property that you're negotiating on in the neighborhood. We call these "ghost signs," and again, they're a great way to test the market and build a buyers' list. Make a sign just like the one above, advertising the terms you expect to offer on a slow flip. When someone calls, you can say, "I'm sorry, but that house just sold. But I get ones just like it all the time. Let me jot down your information, and as soon as the next one comes up, I'll call you to come to take a look at it."

Before long, you'll have 200 to 250 names and numbers for people who are interested in an owner-financed house for $3,000 or $5,000 down, no credit check. This is an effective strategy that costs almost nothing. It builds your buyers' list, which is key for filling slow flips quickly, and it builds your confidence as an investor. I've been at this for decades. I know my market, and I know that I can sell beat-up houses with owner financing and $4,000 down, no credit check, all day long. But if you're new to this, getting those calls and seeing the concrete demand for what you'll be selling offers great comfort.

Facebook Marketplace

Facebook marketplace has become an invaluable tool for filling slow flips. It has a wide reach, and it's free, with good results, requiring minimal work on your part. I'll talk about several ways that we use Facebook Marketplace to fill houses.

First, we can use this site the same way we use signs. If like me, you're no tech expert, you can think of Facebook Marketplace and similar platforms as essentially electronic signs with some snazzy features that make them easier to use. One big advantage of this platform is that, unlike ghost signs, you don't have to be in the location you're testing. Someone has to drive around and post the physical signs we discussed above, but you can be three states over—or halfway around the world—and test a market with ghost ads. In fact, running ghost ads in various places is a great way to gauge what market you want to be in if you live somewhere too expensive for slow flipping.

As with our for-sale signs, you can create a Facebook Marketplace listing advertising the general terms of a slow flip that you have not yet closed on. Simply, go to Facebook Marketplace online, and under "Categories," in the left-hand column, click on "Home Sales." Click on + **Create new listing** at the top left of your screen and enter the info as directed. You can give the general location for a property you're working on (no specific address, since you don't yet own it), condition, and the terms of a sale—$3,000 down, $875 a month with owner financing, no credit check, or whatever.

You can follow the same steps to create "ghost ads" that will allow you to gauge your local market or a long-distance market that interests you even if you aren't yet working on a specific property there. Enter basic info and the neighborhood in various ads, leaving out the addresses. As responses come in, keep track of interested parties and build your buyers' list.

You might think to yourself, "I'm interested in St. Louis or central Ohio, Nebraska, or Indianapolis." Start testing specific areas. If one spot gets five responses and another gets 75, that's an easy choice. Go where you see demand. This is a good strategy for readers in California, Seattle, Brooklyn, and Colorado—places that don't have deals. As I've said, I always recommend staying in your own market if you can. Most people can buy locally, at least within a few hours of where they live. Others, though, live in markets where they can't buy, and this is a great way to get a feel for the places where they might want to invest.

My recommendation, as I said earlier, is to pick just one market if you're investing over a long distance, and focus on that spot. We were talking with Shlomo this week, the investor living in Israel who I earlier mentioned working with. He's buying in Ohio, so it's very long-distance, but all his properties are in that state, not scattered throughout the U.S. This approach makes things much easier because you can have one agent that you work with, one person putting on your lock boxes and taking your videos, one person doing your court filings—potentially, one person filling all of those roles. If you're in 20 different markets, even if they're all healthy, you have to have people all over the place to do these chores. Just sticking out a batch of signs becomes a hassle, with multiple people to contact and check up on. You also get to know the ins and outs of a particular market over time, and that's always helpful.

Testing demand in a market is a vital complement to our strategies for finding slow flips. There are areas with plenty of deals available, but they might be suffering from population decline or severe economic distress and have very low demand. The smart investor gets a feel for both sides of the equation—the supply of and demand for affordable houses—before plunging into a market.

Before we move on to making Facebook Marketplace ads for the properties you have closed on, I want to tell a story that highlights how ghost ads can turn into real money. I work with a woman who lives in Texas and buys in Alabama. She had a property pending on contract there, but she was nervous, as anybody would be, so she wanted to run some test ads to gauge the marketplace. She was buying the house really cheap, for $15,000, and wanted to sell it with owner financing for $60,000. She put it out there on Facebook Marketplace for all these investors, using the actual property address but saying clearly, we have not closed on it yet. Well, from those ads, she ended up getting a cash offer for $50,000. She closed and then took that offer, opting to put around $35,000 in her pocket and not keep the property as a slow flip. This wasn't the original plan, but running ghost ads provided her with an outcome she was thrilled with.

When I advertise an actual property that I have closed, I always want to cut down on the number of calls I'm getting and the number of back-and-forth coming from Facebook Marketplace. Tools like this should save you time, not cost you more, and it's easy to get sucked into hours of fielding queries that go nowhere if you don't approach this marketing the right way.

One way to cut down on phone time and questions is to be as detailed and concrete as you can in your Facebook Marketplace ads. I want to include all the info in my ad and a link to a video in which I do a thorough walkthrough or have someone I hired do one. We want to show everything we can in that video. Your instinct might be to soft-peddle problems with a house. Don't do it! Be honest and don't hide anything. Covering up problems will only hurt you in the end. If you have a leak or a hole in the ceiling, don't skip it, thinking I don't want them to see that. Yes, you do! Because guess what? They're going to see it anyway. I do the opposite. I like to zoom in on the problems and let them know, "Hey, looks like there's a leak up here; there's a hole over there. We don't know what the problem is. We haven't done a professional inspection, but we noticed this and want you to know about it." Reveal everything negative about the house. If the floor is uneven and you can't see that with a camera, you can say it on the video: where I'm standing here, the floors are a little soft, or they feel uneven.

I want potential buyers to make a clear assessment and good decision based on that video. If after watching the video and seeing the entire house's flaws, people still want to see it. I'll let them in. This approach cuts out all sorts of people who want to move into a ready, well-maintained house. Well, if you're not handy or don't have access to someone who is, my house probably isn't for you. Many people will realize this with a clear ad and video, and click the "back" button instead of wasting their time on the phone. Other potential buyers will think, "Here's a deal. That plumbing issue or new drywall would cost a fortune with a contractor (no wonder the price is so low), but I can do this work myself. This is a great property where I can add value and turn a profit."

We use Craigslist in the same way that we use Facebook Marketplace. Craigslist used to be our number-one online source until Facebook came along. One reason I like Facebook Marketplace is that it gives you some insight into the people you're communicating with. When people send you messages, you can look back at them and see their page and maybe some work they've done. You get a sense of whom you're talking to. Are they investors doing a lot of deals? What kind? You get a read on people and how serious they are, and, of course, this goes both ways. They get to see you and look at what you've done and what you're working on. This can be hard when you're starting, obviously, and don't have much of a track record. Later, we'll talk about some things you can do to boost your social proof and give you more credibility. For now, just keep in mind that this read of another person goes both ways. You want to look friendly and professional on Facebook, not like some hooligan running around and partying. Assume that everyone you're dealing with will look you up online and if you have pages to clean up, get to it. This isn't true of Craigslist. You remain anonymous when you place ads there. We still use it, as I said, but that anonymity lowers comfort levels, and it's one of the reasons that Facebook Marketplace gets much better results.

Automation, My Deal Factory

I hope that you can see by now why I devoted an entire chapter—the first chapter of the book, no less—to creating a vision and establishing your freedom number. It isn't just some feel-good exercise. It's the heart of your business plan. You now know exactly how many slow flips you're aiming for. After deciding on the number of slow flips they need, however, some readers will feel overwhelmed. How am I supposed to do five, 10, or 20 of these while working a full-time job? Don't worry, it's absolutely manageable. I've spent years developing a system that minimizes work and stress, partly by relying heavily on automation.

Let me remind you that at the time of this writing, I have 138 properties, all slow flips, with 20 more under contract. How many employees does that take? None. I have one person who is an employee of another company doing some work for me part-time. Other than that, I handle everything, and I do it without breaking a sweat. I have a solid system in place that maximizes efficiency, and automation takes care of much of what needs doing. I'm not exaggerating when I say that my hardest job at this point is cashing checks.

I don't have anyone answering the phone or handling repair calls because we don't do repairs. Remember that in the slow flip, you're not a landlord. Our paperwork is simple, and our formula for buying and selling reduces everything to basic math. Certain tasks do need to be performed, and for those, we outsource everything we can.

Deal Factory, www.mydealfactory.com, has become a vital part of the formula for me. Don't forget the "my" in that Web address and don't confuse Deal Factory with "Deal Machine," another helpful app we talked about in Chapter 3. I use Deal Factory for a dozen different things, but here, I want to focus on how I use it to fill slow flip properties.

Generally speaking, Deal Factory is what MBA types call CRM, or Customer Relationship Management software. It helps you manage contacts and leads and follow up with prospects. It allows you to track conversations and painlessly send email blasts and mass texts. For our purposes, filling slow flips, Deal Factory's greatest benefit is that it easily allows you to use a different phone number for each property.

Distinct phone numbers are important for lots of reasons. One of the biggest is that they hugely cut down on your phone time. Without this kind of system, you'll spend a painful amount of time on the phone; most of it wasted on aimless calls. Anyone who has ever advertised anything on Facebook Marketplace knows what I'm talking about. You place an ad saying:

House for sale

123 Main St.

$3,000 down, $875 a month - owner financing

3 beds, 1 bath

Needs work

Guess what the first person who calls from the ad will say ...

"Hi, I'm calling about your ad in the Facebook marketplace?"

"Yes," you reply, "What can I help you with?"

"I see here, it says three bedrooms?"

"Yep, it's three bedrooms."

"And one bath?"

"Yeah, there's one bath."

"And it's $3,000 down, $875 a month?"

"Yup."

"That's with owner financing?"

"Yes, it is."

"Yeah, okay, I'm gonna think about it. Thank you."

You say to yourself, "What just happened here?" This person called me and literally just read the ad. Sometimes, they ask, "How much is it down?" In a fit of annoyance, I'll be a wise guy and say, "Hang on, let me check the ad." "Well, it says here in the ad that it's $3,000 down, $875 a month." This phenomenon of calling to read the ad back must be human nature because everyone does it, but I can't waste my day on these kinds of conversations. After a while, you don't even want to answer your phone. You have 100 people calling and asking the same thing, and all the answers are in front of them.

Deal Factory lets us get around this hassle by assigning a unique phone number to each property. Each number is temporary and only works until your slow flip is filled. When our curious friends call up to recite the ad back line by line, they get a specific voicemail for the house they're calling on:

The property that you are calling about, for sale at 123 Main St., has 3 bedrooms, 1 bath, and needs work. The owner will finance the purchase, with $3,000 down and $875 a month. Please drive by the property to see it, and if you're still interested, call (Google Voice number here). Thank you.

I always give the address because they might have seen a sign that was not in front of the house (we stick them throughout the neighborhood) and be unsure of the location after jotting down a phone number. They also might be calling on a dozen houses, and I want to make sure they're clear about which one is mine.

As with Facebook Marketplace ads, we want to be completely honest in all our marketing, including these voicemail messages. If the house is a "handyman special," say so. If it has no kitchen, no appliances, if it's full of garbage or leaking like a sieve, say so. There's a limit to what you can say in a short voicemail but don't sugarcoat anything. A clear voicemail message and an honest description will eliminate many buyers who actually want a house in better condition, meaning they're not real prospects for you, but timewasters. You want to discourage them.

If buyers call my Google Voice number after hearing the voicemail message for the property, I immediately ask if they've driven there and seen it in person yet. If they haven't, I insist that they do so before we go any further. "I want you to do your own due diligence," I say. "Drive over to 123 Main St. Feel free to walk around the property and look in the windows. If you're still interested, call me back."

If you haven't used them, Google Voice numbers are reliable—they work on smart phones through the Web and aren't tied to one device. They're good for blocking spam, and calls can be forwarded. These numbers can be easily switched out for new ones, and they help decide who can reach you and when.

In addition to having a separate voicemail for each property, Deal Factory captures the phone numbers of every person calling those distinct numbers. It doesn't matter if they end up being your buyers or even connect with you; you get their numbers and know that they called about the house at 123 Main St., selling for $3,000 down and $875 a month.

I absolutely love this feature! After running an ad, you have all of these numbers captured—50, 200, or 400. Now, you have the ability to send out one mass text with info on that property to everyone who called about it. When that property closes, you could have a list of 500 people who might be interested in your next one, which is in a similar price range, $4,000 down, $875 a month, etc. Some of those people will have already found a property and will tell you to take them off your list. Great, you want them off your list because they're no longer in the market. Others will still be looking, and others will be investors who are always buying. They can stay on your list long-term.

The point is, with hundreds of high-quality leads like this, you might not need any other marketing—no cumbersome signs or online ads to find buyers for the next house. This is a fantastic, efficient way to fill slow flips. The software does the heavy lifting for you. You simply respond with one text or one ringless voicemail. I usually send a mass text from that number and say something like:

New property for sale, 123 Main St., $5,000 down $875, a month, 3 beds, 2 baths, needs work. Call 555-1000.

I send out that text to my list of several hundred numbers. The contact number in that text is a second number within the system, and when prospects call it, they'll get a voice message giving them all the details on that specific property. The ways that Deal Factory helps you track and manage these calls and harness them for marketing saves massive amounts of time, boosts efficiency, and helps you stay organized. It increases your marketing muscle with a simple, low-cost tech solution.

Get a Website

Having some sort of website is important for filling your properties for two reasons. The first is your credibility. In discussing Facebook Marketplace, I said one reason it works so well is that potential buyers and investors can see who you are and assess your credibility. How do you gain credibility when you haven't done much or any investing? Well, having a website is a must.

Years ago, if you had a website, it was a big thing. People were immediately impressed. The technology was relatively new, and websites were expensive to build. Now, anybody can get a website. You can even get a very basic one for free at sites like www.Weebly.com and www.Wix.com, or upgrade to a better one for cheap. If you're tech-savvy, you might be able to design and maintain your own site. The technology has gotten more user-friendly, and several vendors follow a do-it-yourself model, with professional-looking templates and options. This all means that the bar has shifted. Having a website is no longer impressive, but not having one peg you as an amateur and a dabbler. It's a bottom-line, price-of-admission item you must have to be taken seriously.

Your website doesn't have to have many frills or be fancy, but you do need the basics on there, and you want it to be optimized, meaning you can be found online. Sites like www.Wix.com and www.Weebly.com will optimize your site, and they have a variety of packages and upgrades available.

We use a $99 program available from Carrot, www.bestinvestorsites.com, which promotes its custom websites as "lead generation hubs," superior to websites. These are websites, whatever Carrot's marketing pitch, but they're designed for real estate investors and have some very nice features that suit our needs. The $99 "Content Pro" package we buy includes content marketing and SEO (search engine optimization) tools and gives you three separate websites. In terms of slow flipping, we use one of those websites for filling properties—our houses are offered for sale with owner financing. We upload the details, photos, videos, etc. when we want to market houses and then take that content down once they're filled. We use a second Carrot website to promote our "we buy houses" business, searching for slow flips, as well as houses for wholesaling, which isn't covered in this book. We highlight the fact that we'll pay cash for a distressed house "as is," with no cleanup, marketing, or sales commissions necessary. We offer a quick, easy exit, and no house is too ugly or dilapidated.

You don't need a Carrot site starting; a free one will do. When you start turning over several properties, the Carrot sites are helpful because you can put up all the information on your property and then make it invisible—just flip a switch—after you find a buyer. If that person moves out or an investor-buyer turns the property back over to you, you can click on the listing and turn that property back on, with all the saved info.

When you meet with somebody, this will be the first thing they ask you, "What's your web address?" Yes, anyone can get one now, without paying a dime, but people still use it to gauge who you are. You must have a website. If you don't, you look like you aren't real, and you don't exist, as far as others are concerned. Make sure to put your web address on your business cards too. Half the time someone asks for a card these days, it's so that they can see your website. Quick, easy sites like the ones available at Wix, Weebly, and Carrot have been really effective for us, as well as easy to put together and maintain.

My Showing System

I've mentioned that I run my business—138 slow flips and counting, as I write this—with no full-time employee, partly because I have systems in place to automate and save time. My system for showing houses to prospective buyers is a prime example. Some readers whose freedom numbers were in the range of 20 or more slow flips are probably daunted by the idea of showing all those properties. But even three or four can seem overwhelming if you don't have an efficient system.

I do have an efficient system, and it has worked like a charm for the last decade. Before I describe it, I should say in advance that some readers would absolutely hate it. Some of you will say Scott's out of his mind. I'm tossing this book across the room. I understand your skepticism, but let me say again, this system has worked incredibly well for me for 10 years, without a single problem. I'm well aware that I could have a problem with it someday, but even if that happens, it will be well worth the tradeoff, given the amount of time and effort it has saved.

Now that I've prepared you, here goes ...

As soon as I close on a house, I put a lockbox on it (that's usually the last time I see the property). Many readers are familiar with this device, which works like a mini-safe with a key locked safely inside. The lockbox looks like a giant padlock and locks onto a doorknob. Most have a keypad or the kinds of tumblers you see on bike combination locks. Put in the right code, and a visitor can slide over a panel and get to the key inside. The visitor opens the house door and then puts the key back in the lockbox, which slides shut and can't be opened again until the next visitor punches in the code. There are some very fancy high-tech lockboxes on the market now, but for our purposes, I recommend a cheap basic model.

When a buyer or investor-buyer finally says, "Yes, I've seen the house and I'm interested," I make sure they really have driven by the property and walked around. I won't deal with them until they do. Often, they'll say, "I'm here at the house right now. I see it. I like it. When can you come out and show me the inside?" I always reply, "I'm available anytime, no problem at all. Just let me know an hour in advance. If it turns out I can't make it, I have a next-door neighbor with a key who can open it up and let you in."

Note that I am not giving them a time or schedule a showing. I never do. I say, "Anytime is fine. Just call me one hour in advance. I have a neighbor with a key. If for some reason I'm tied up, he'll open the door for you." That's how I leave it.

The prospective buyer calls the next morning at 10 a.m. and says, "You told me to call you an hour in advance. I'll be there at 11." I tell them, "Okay, great. I should be able to make it but if not, don't worry, my neighbor will let you in."

I have them call an hour in advance not because I'm heading out to the property, but so that I know to pay attention to my phone. I don't want to miss the call if someone has driven out there and is standing on my front porch, phoning to say, "Here I am." When they arrive and don't see anyone, they call, of course, and I say, "I'm tied up, and my neighbor just stepped out, but since you're there, I'm going to go ahead and give you the code for the lockbox. You can let you let yourself in. If my neighbor shows up, just tell him you know me and I gave you the code to check the place out."

I usually stay on the phone with them while they open the lockbox and get the key since some have never used one. I describe the device—it looks like a big padlock on the front door—and tell them the code to dial in. Okay, there's a little black tab to the left. Push the tab down the front of the box and open it to get the key. Open the house door. Put the key back in the box, and spin the dial to jumble the combination.

If buyers call back and say, "Okay, we like it. What's the next step?" I ask them to text me their full names and all their information, and then meet me at the office with the down payment. I'll do the paperwork before they get there. If they don't want the house, I never have to see or speak to them again, period. That's absolutely fine. They move on, and I have not wasted any time.

Some of my students hate this idea when they first hear it. They immediately think that the buyer you gave the code is going to steal your fridge, trash the place, or throw a party. How do you know they won't do X or take Y? You don't. Although the house is in many cases already trashed or in disrepair, there's always something to steal or damage. It could happen, but in 10 years, I've never had a problem, and I've used the same code on every house for almost all that time. I used to use different codes and keep a list, but I would inevitably forget them or the list. I'd get locked out of my own house and have to throw away a lockbox and start again.

At this point, whenever I do seminars, someone asks, "What happened to the neighbor who was supposed to help you?" To be clear, there is no neighbor. I made him up. I could just give a buyer the code over the phone in advance and say, "Let yourself in," but in the wrong hands, that does seem like an invitation to robbery or vandalism.

Someone might show up with a van and three friends, knowing in advance that he's being given access and a self-guided tour. The way I do it, they don't know they'll be let in alone until they're on the porch. They're a little taken by surprise; they appreciate the trust, and they think there's a watchful neighbor who could be back any minute.

Why do I run showings this way? For one thing, you can do this sort of showing at any time, as long as you have a working phone turned on. You can do it from across the country or the world. The bigger reason—and readers who have rentals know this all too well—is that when you say you'll see buyers there in person at 11 a.m., some will take one look at the exterior and walk away. Some won't even get out of the car. Buyers think, *"There's no way I would live here,"* or an investor thinks, *"I don't want properties in this area,"* and we think—in great frustration—that's why we insisted you drive by the house first, which is something you apparently didn't do.

Many other potential buyers, a disturbingly high percentage, as the landlords among you know, will set an appointment and simply not show up. You drive out there to meet them, or if you're working a distant market, send someone, and they just don't bother. No call or text, just a no-show. Before I moved to my current system, I tried to schedule 10 to 20 buyers for the same time. Maybe three out of 20 would show up—a terrible percentage—but at least, the trips weren't a complete waste of my time.

My current system works much better. The only time I meet with buyers is if they want to purchase the property. If you're only doing one slow flip and you're lonely, maybe you want to drive to the house repeatedly to chat with buyers. But if you're doing any kind of volume at all, you have to start assigning a value to your time, an actual dollar amount. Your time really is money. Even a few slow flips can mean dozens of wasted trips to show houses, and that's time that could be spent building your business.

Justifying Value

Buyers who are interested after touring a house might want to discuss how you arrived at the price and what the real value is. We touched on the idea of how value is created earlier in the book, but I want to explore it in more depth here because it's a fundamental principle of slow flipping. Many readers are probably still wondering how we can justify the value of a distressed house at $89,000 when we bought it for $30,000 and did nothing to improve it.

Your buyers might wonder about this too. First, never try to justify your price or convince anyone of the value. Let them make their own decisions. As I've noted, buyers inevitably will come to you and say, "We spotted a house on the next block or three doors down from yours that's only $40,000. Yours is $89,000."

I immediately agree with them that the other house sounds like a great deal. "If you like it," I say, "you should probably buy that one."

"Well, we can't buy that one," they reply. "We called the owner, and he said he'll only take cash for it."

"Well, then maybe you should buy mine because here, you only need $3,000 down."

I'm always brutally honest. Don't be embarrassed about this. Don't be afraid. I say straight out, if they like that other house or the other price better, they should buy it. I would if I were they. And then, trust me, they're going to tell you why they can't buy that one and why they have to buy yours. Leave the ball in their court. Make it their decision. It makes them feel in control—which they are, of course—but it also gives you much more control than if you enter into some sort of contest, trying to justify your price. You're not trying to hide anything or talk up your house. You do not want to reply, "Well, mine's better because I have 20 more square feet," or "I have a driveway, and they don't." Don't get into any of that.

Some potential buyers will realize the key thing your house has that the other one doesn't—yours is a real possibility for them, given their finances. Some people will move on, of course, which is fine. Some will be annoyed that you don't want to haggle or get into some deep comparison that might drive the price down. Often, they'll say, "That's never going to work. You'll never get $5,000 down or $89,000 ... This will never sell for $110,000."

I've been at this a long time, and I always say, calmly, with a smile, "This house will be sold in a week. No question about it. It doesn't have to be sold to you." Simple as that. I never argue with anybody. I never try to convince them or prove my point. This is the deal that I'm offering. If you want it, great. If not, lots of other houses out there.

Buyers who mention another cheaper house but then talk themselves into yours come to realize something, whether or not they think of it in these terms: we sell financing, and the house comes with it. What they're really buying is the opportunity for homeownership. No matter their credit rating, employment history, or bank balance, they have the chance to own a house with your offer of owner financing. All they need is a $3,000 down payment and $875 a month. They can't get a bank loan, but they can swing this. You've opened a door for them, just as, years ago, that door was opened for me.

Remember those non-qualifying assumptions I described in Chapter 1? I was thrilled with them because they gave me the chance to buy houses in the only way I could. I never had appraisals or home inspections. I never looked at comparable properties to see what anything was worth. I'm not saying this was right or wrong. All I knew back then was that for $3,000 down, $2,000, or $5,000—whatever the deal was—I could buy a house. And I could make a small profit on the rent I got from it after paying my mortgage each month. That was all I knew and all I cared about. That's how I bought then, and that's how I sell today. You'll see the same idea at work all over, now that you're thinking about it, for instance, at car lots. You will notice cars advertised now for $500 down, $225 a month, or whatever. Sometimes, they don't even mention the price. They're taking the exact same approach, selling for an amount down and a manageable amount per month. They're buying cars for $1,000 and selling them for $5,000 because all you need to buy one is $500 down and $225 a month. People are thrilled with that offer because they're buying the financing—the cars come with it.

If somebody has a problem with your terms, fine, they're not your buyer. You don't need them. This is the great thing about real estate. You have a house and a pool of potential buyers. But you don't need all of those buyers to like your deal, just one. One house, one person. This business is a very different sort of business from a hamburger stand, where you need thousands of people to come in and want your product.

You must please them all. In slow flipping, you don't have to please everybody. One house has to work for one buyer.

Another response you can give people concerned about value and how you arrived at your $89,000 or $110,000 price tag is that a thing is worth whatever someone is willing to pay for it. This might sound like a jokey answer, but it's actually a fundamental principle of economics. It's how markets work. The price of anything is "whatever the market will bear," as the well-worn phrase goes. Often, I have a couple sitting in the office, and when they ask about the price and how I figured it, I'm honest. We make up the price. It's based on what we think the market will bear. This is the price because someone is willing to pay $89,000 for this house. The person doesn't have to be you. I then point to the wife's handbag. Sometimes, it's a Louis Vuitton. Sometimes, it's from Target.

"Look at that pocketbook," I say. "If you buy one that size from Louis Vuitton, it might be $2,500. Buy it from Walmart, and it is $25. Same size purse, with similar pockets. Both carry your keys, phone, and wallet. Both zip up and have shoulder straps. The value is based on what someone is willing to pay. Lots of people want the Walmart one, but plenty of buyers are lining up for the Louis Vuitton too."

That's the only way I justify value. Someone is willing to pay $89,000 for my house and will shortly. That person does not have to be you.

Now, clearly, we want to structure deals so that they work for our buyers, too. Sometimes, they plan to rent the houses out or rehab and resell them. Our offer of owner financing allows them to do that. If we turned $30,000 into $90,000, that shouldn't affect their ability to further profit from a house if they're smart about it. You want them to be smart about it, and you want them to turn a profit because your buyers are your clients. They're your customers, not your adversaries, and I hope I didn't imply that with my frank talk about value. In that instance, I'm simply being honest, not trying to goad buyers. You don't want to butt heads with them or get into antagonistic relationships. Whenever possible, you want to cultivate, train, and help them. The better your buyers do, the more money they make, the more money you make, and the more business they want to do with you.

If a buyer has a problem, you want to help them through that problem whenever possible. Remember, in a sense, they're working for you in your role as Mr. Burns. They are doing all the work, cleaning up, making repairs, fixing air conditioners, collecting rent, going to court, etc. They do all of that so that they can send you money. They are on your team, and you want them to do well. You want them to make money because they're making it for you, and if things work out, many buyers will make you more money in the future. You want buyers saying, "This was a good deal. Let me know when you have another house available." I constantly get texts from my buyers, saying, "Let me know when you get another property."

I often think about my regular buyers' business plans and how a property might work for them when I'm buying a slow flip. This was true of a house I bought recently for a little more than usual. I got it for about $45,000 and paid cash because I'd just closed on another deal and had $90,000 sitting in the account. This one was intriguing to me because it's a big house, with seven bedrooms. I debated a lot about how much I would charge, but I knew it would be a significant amount because I have many buyers who purchase my houses and then rent out rooms, some for $600 to $700 a month. Before I even bought this house, I was doing the math on their end, thinking, "Cool, they're going to make $4,000 a month off this house. Clearly, they can afford to pay me $1,500." That's a lot more than I collect on the average slow flip house, as you know, but the point is, I was thrilled to have a house that I knew one of my regular buyers could make a killing off later. I am happy to see them turn a profit, and I always want to leave room for that. You should never feel resentful that someone is making a lot of money, maybe even more than you are, from your slow flip. Never count the money in another person's pocket. You might already think this way, but if not, you have to adjust your mindset. If you operate on the principle that it's never okay to leave a dollar on the table, you're in the wrong business. Always leave something for the next guy.

I understand that if you're collecting checks of $800 a month on a property and your buyer is making $3,000 a month from it, you might be tempted to resent them or feel like you made a mistake. You should have charged more or structured things differently or kept that house and rented out rooms yourself. Don't think that way. First, the whole point of slow flipping is not to be a landlord. Your buyers who are crushing it and making $3,000 a month off a house you slow flipped are working hard for that money, dealing with repairs, vacancies, evictions, and all manner of headaches that you're avoiding. You want them to be handsomely rewarded for that work, so they keep doing it and sending you checks. You want them to feel like you empowered them. Celebrate their success. I mean that sincerely. It's another case of real estate karma. Get into the mindset that you want everybody around you to make more money. The more money they make, the more money you make. Trust me on this. When other people do well, celebrate them and be happy for them. You'll be surprised at the various ways it will come back to benefit you later.

By now, you should have a good grasp of strategies for finding and marketing slow flip houses. Then what? In the next chapter, we'll get down to the nitty-gritty process of closing the deal with your buyers, from qualifying them and negotiating (I don't do either) to filling out paperwork (I keep it very simple). We'll also tackle follow-ups, things like receiving payment and getting online reviews once a successful deal is finished.

5

Closing Slow Flips

Closing a slow flip deal can get an investor's heart racing, which is understandable, especially if they've never done it before. The terms alone—*qualifying buyers, insurance policies, and signing contracts*—are enough to make you sweat. Well, relax! I've done hundreds of these over the years, and in this chapter, I'll show you how I've simplified the process. Qualifying buyers can get extremely complicated, so as I'll explain shortly, we don't do it. Negotiating over price is stressful, so we don't do that either. "Signing contracts" makes everyone, especially your customers, nervous, so instead, we "approve agreements." Those agreements are solid but simple, and once you have a good one, no lawyer is required.

Closing a deal should be a clean, easy process, and more than that, a happy, even inspirational one. You're giving an individual a shot at homeownership or an investor the chance to build their income. In this chapter, we'll explore the steps to getting to a smooth closing and keeping it simple once you're there. We'll also cover follow-up items like accepting cash payments, insurance strategies, and getting reviewed for your successful deals (yes, even the closing becomes a marketing tool in our slow flip system).

Ugly House = You're Lucky!

As you know by now, the slow flip formula calls for buying a "distressed" house and selling it as is. For us, "as is" means just that we don't clean, paint, or re-carpet, and we certainly don't make repairs. Buyers generally understand that they're getting a deal because the house needs a lot of work, and we've already discussed how to explain the value to those who don't. But once you have buyers ready to talk about closing, some will try to prod you into cleanup first.

"What about all the beer bottles? You're gonna clean those out? That paint is peeling off the ceiling; are you going to take care of that?"

My answer to these queries is always the same, "No, I am not going to clean up, and you're lucky we haven't already. Right now, the house is $3,000 down. If I clean it out, the guy I use will charge me $2,000, and then, I have to get a $5,000 down payment." I know you can probably clean this up for a couple of hundred bucks. A friend with a truck, a high school kid helping out, you'll have it looking pretty good inside a week. Wouldn't you rather save the $2,000?

That faulty plumbing, the trashed kitchen, the overgrown swamp in the back yard? I could have taken care of that stuff, but it would add $10,000 or $12,000 to the price. You're getting an incredible deal because this stuff hasn't been fixed. There are other houses in the neighborhood fully repaired and beautifully cleaned, offered through realtors. Look at their prices and then let me know if you'd really want this one cleaned up. The house is $3,000 down and $875 a month as is, but if you want repairs, the price rises substantially.

Immediately, buyers respond with a note of panic, "No, no, we'll take care of it. Don't do anything!" That response, "*You're lucky. You know why?*" completely changes the dynamic. They start thinking they're going to negotiate with you before closing because of the condition. You're informing them that all price adjustments have already been made. The price is already in the basement, with favorable terms for a buyer who has no credit because of the peeling paint and beer bottles. Go check out fully repaired and staged houses if you think you can buy one.

The mental calculus quickly changes, and they realize they are lucky to be getting a low price and owner financing, and that's the case because the house needs real work. Promise me that if you take nothing else from the book, you'll write down that one phrase: "you're lucky." It has the power to change things instantly.

If you doubt this distressed-house dynamic, look at the property pictured below.

This was a house I bought years ago. The one I thought, "Oh crap we actually are going to have to clean this place out" when I took possession. There's no way I can sell this as it sits. The previous owner, I'm guessing, was maybe scamming the newspaper company, pretending to deliver papers while they stacked up in the house, right to the ceiling. I don't clean up houses if I can avoid it, and this was looking like quite a job. I was a little stressed over it, and then, I thought, "I'm at the house anyway. I might as well stick some signs out front."

Within a day, I had two people fighting over the house; one literally cried that she couldn't get it. The first person to put the money in my hand got the house. The other lady ended up getting another house we had, and she's still with us today. The point is that though it is in an abominable condition, two people were fighting over it. The woman who bought it had other rentals on the block. She knew she could clean the house up herself for cheap, and she knew the rent she could get for it once she did.

We rarely do any kind of cleanup—the cans in the cupboard, beer bottles, peeling paint, ratty carpet, or mouse poops all stay. This is how we sell them, and plenty of buyers not only want them like that, they feel lucky to get them.

Sometimes, a property will have citations from the city or the owner is being sued by the municipality for violations. We buy houses like this all the time. We don't fix them or address the violations but simply disclose those problems to our buyers. You must disclose all violations that you should know about. I say to the buyer, "Here's the list from the city. All of this has to be taken care of before anyone can move in." After we buy the place, I put my buyer in touch with the proper city inspector to address the problems.

For readers used to other segments of the market, this dynamic can be hard to believe, but with slow flips, we're in the bargain basement. Think of those stores selling goods that are marked down because there's some flaw or the style is dated or whatever. Consumers attack those racks like piranhas, and it's not unusual to see a fight break out over some flawed item going for cheap. The same principle is in play here, only with houses.

A while back, we had several vacant properties to fill, all but one in pretty bad shape. The horrible houses filled right away. I had one house in good shape, and that was the one I couldn't fill. I didn't understand it. We joked about kicking holes in the walls because the messed-up houses sold so quickly. What was going on? We eventually realized after probing buyers that when the houses were in poor shape, with rotten wood, peeling paint, and bags of clothes in the bedrooms, people understood why they had the opportunity—low money down, low payments, and no credit check. When the house looked perfect, they started thinking, "This can't be right. What's the scam here? What am I not seeing?"

As ironic as it sounds, I have way better luck with distressed properties than I do with houses that look good. This is the opposite of most real estate, but with slow flips, the houses that need significant work go faster and easier than the nice ones.

Below is a photo of the worst house I ever bought, which is saying something, since I've picked up some real wrecks over the years. I wouldn't normally buy a place in this condition. I aim for houses that need work but are livable or just about livable. If I'd gone inside this house, I probably wouldn't have bought it for $5,000.

I wound up with this place because it was part of a package. I bought some houses together from someone I knew and crushed the deal. The houses came to something like $22,000 each. When I finally sent over a guy to do a video of this one, he said, "Did you know that house had a fire?"

"No, I did not." I was somewhat mad since I knew the seller and he never told me about any fire. In fairness, I'd bought the whole package without looking at all the interiors. I knew the neighborhood well and knew the seller, so I did drive-bys but no real due diligence. Anyway, the deal worked out so well for me financially. I figured that even if I had to give this one away, I would still be way ahead.

I told my guy, "Go ahead and stick some signs out anyway; I'll probably just give the place away." To my amazement, we sold the house immediately to a contractor. I priced it lower than usual, I think, for $55,000, with $2,000 down and a payment of $575 a month. That's low, but not bad, considering that I was willing to give it away. The contractor fixed it up beautifully, repaired the damage, and renovated the whole place. He made money off the deal, and he paid me off about a year ago.

So, even this house, literally the worst one I've ever sold, turned into decent money. Below is a picture of how it looked after the renovation.

Qualifying Buyers and Approving Agreements

This section on dealing with buyers could be a book in itself, but I will simply touch on two things here—the process of qualifying buyers and the "contract" you have them "sign" (we'll get to specific paperwork in the next section).

Once buyers have seen that ad, toured the house, and decided they want to buy, how do you qualify them? The term itself sounds complicated, and if you've ever taken out a bank loan, qualifying can be. Institutional lenders have turned it into a science, with complex software and financial checks involved, so how do I, as an individual investor, qualify buyers? The short answer is, "I don't."

Let me explain. You have a property listed on your website. You created Facebook Marketplace ads, posted horrible signs, sent out marketing blasts through My Deal Factory, and people called. They've seen your property, and multiple parties were interested. How do you pick one? Who should you allow to buy the house? I simply do it on a first-come-first-served basis. The first buyer who has the down payment, who can make the first month's mortgage payment, and who wants the property gets the property.

This is not the only way to do it, but I think it's the simplest. Anti-discrimination laws in housing are powerful and often, complicated. You never under any circumstance want to be seen as discriminating, and showing any kind of preference in a sale can look like discrimination from a legal standpoint, though that might not be your intention. I've been investing in real estate for most of my adult life, and even for me, following all these anti-discrimination rules to the letter, without any inadvertent violation, can be tough. But if you always take the very first person who has the dough and wants the house, you're safe. It protects you, and it speeds up the process.

Now, we are asking for a down payment of several thousand dollars, so that in itself is a kind of qualification and should give you some comfort. Whoever is buying the house, at least 99 percent of the time, will have to do some serious work on it, which also provides comfort. I figure, if they default, that's okay. I obviously don't want them to default, but if someone can no longer pay the mortgage, well, they had a shot and they move along. They probably will have cleaned the house up or made some repairs while they were in it. You keep that first down payment, find another buyer who gives you a new down payment, and start over. By the way, plenty of people who couldn't qualify on paper, according to the usual standards, will surprise you. They're happy to have a shot at homeownership. They'll make every effort to get payments in on time and work at improving the property. I know because I was one of those people.

If you remember my story from Chapter 1, you'll recall that I started with "non-qualifying" assumptions. As I explained early in the book, that meant I was taking over existing mortgages to buy houses and didn't have to qualify in any way—no credit check, employment history, and bank statements. That's what "non-qualifying" means. Remember, I was mowing lawns for a living then. I had bad credit and no real job, yet I was able to buy all those houses. I was ambitious, and non-qualifying deals gave me a shot, and so, moving forward, I sort of feel like, who am I to tell people they can't buy a house without good credit or a good job? I have the right to do that, but I don't want to. Call it real estate karma.

I give people the same opportunity now that I had back then. I don't ask about jobs or credit or bank accounts. As long as they have the down payment and accept our terms, they're qualified.

You might not be comfortable with that approach. If that idea scares you or you're thinking, "There is no way I am letting somebody come in without screening them or prequalifying them," you can establish standards. But they have to be concrete, and you must put them in writing. This is important, so let me restate it. If you are going to go the other route and qualify your buyers according to certain standards, you must put down in writing your minimum acceptable criteria. That might be a minimum credit score of 620, for instance, a minimum monthly income three times the payment amount, or a criminal record totaling no more than 18 arrests. Whatever your criteria, you must have them written down, and you have to make sure you're using them and only them. Once someone meets your criteria, on the very first instance, they get the deal. I hope this makes sense. You cannot say, "Yes, this guy from yesterday qualifies, but the woman I talked to this morning qualifies better." You can't say, "Yes, that person qualifies," but I'm going to hold out for someone I like better who also qualifies. Anything like that will be seen as discrimination, and you can't do it.

There are things we have wiggle room on when slow flipping—a down payment, interest rate, and the price we'll buy at—but this is not one of those things. You can't have any exceptions, or you're asking for trouble. That's why I simply say that the first person to put the money in my hand gets the house.

Once you have buyers selected, either because they're the first with cash in hand or the first to meet your minimum acceptable criteria, it's time for paperwork. You might have the urge to tell them that it's time to sign a contract since that's what you're doing. Don't! We never "sign," and we never call the paperwork a "contract." Instead, we say, "I just need you to approve the agreement for deed." We are approving an agreement, not signing a contract. Why? When you say the words, "contract" and "sign," buyers' radar immediately switches on. They get nervous and start thinking that they should probably show everything to a lawyer or ask others for advice. *"My brother-in-law's cousin married a lawyer. I wonder if he'd review all this when he has time?"* That little change in wording—approving an agreement, not signing a contract— will get you more on-the-spot contracts and avoid suffering delays or involving the buyer's extended family tree in the transaction. Everything you're doing is legal and above board, but moving quickly with minimal headaches is important for your business model. Keeping things streamlined is best for you and for the buyer, so along with "asking" (as in, asking price), add "contract" and "sign" to the list of words you no longer speak.

Master Land Contract

New investors often think you need to be a lawyer or an accountant to handle the paperwork in a real estate transaction, but the agreement and process we use to close our buyers are simple enough that we can handle it ourselves.

We do what's called a "table closing," meaning a specific time and date is established and the parties meet in person or virtually. If you have an office, the buyers can come in and handle the closing there. If you don't have an office and you're local, you can meet them at the house they're buying or at a coffee shop. If you're working in a distant market, the closing can be handled through DocuSign or another signing app. The very term "closing" might make you nervous, but don't worry, this is easy stuff.

Your buyers might be experienced investors who know the ropes or first-time buyers who are new to this. If they're going to be owner-occupants, it's a good idea to make clear what will happen if they want to leave in 10 or 15 years. The possible scenarios will be the same as if they had their mortgage with Chase or Bank of America. The choices will be:

1. Sell the house and pay me the unpaid balance on the loan.
2. Turn the keys back to me, relinquishing the house.
3. Keep the house and rent it to a tenant who you will collect rent from.

If buyers choose option 1, you do well since you've collected a down payment and monthly payments for some years. And now, you're being paid off on a house worth at least $89,000 when you bought it for $30,000. Option 2 often makes sense for buyers; since even after a decade, they will have built up very little equity in the property. If buyers choose option 3 down the road, they're responsible for the same mortgage payment as always, no matter what the rent is, or whether their tenants pay it or don't. They also remain responsible for all upkeep, maintenance, repairs, etc. You are still just the lender, Mr. Burns up in the corner office. The other possibility would be that buyers could just leave the place vacant and continue making payments, though this seldom happens for more than a brief spell. It's their house, and they're in control, just as they would be with a mortgage from any institutional lender.

Unlike banks, however, we keep the process and paperwork basic. We use what's called an "agreement for deed" or in some states, a "land contract" or "contract for deed." It's all the same, with the same result. Wherever you're located, you should have someone local review a land agreement before you use it to make sure that it complies with your state's laws.

Below is an example of the "agreement for deed" that we use in Virginia.

AGREEMENT FOR DEED

THIS AGREEMENT FOR DEED is made and entered into this _______ day of ________ 20__, by and between, ____________________________ (hereinafter referred to as "First Party"), and ____________ (hereinafter referred to as "Second Party).

WITNESSETH, that if the Second Party shall first make the payments and perform the covenants hereinafter mentioned on his part to be made and performed, the First Party hereby covenants and agrees to convey to the Second Party, his heirs, executors, administrators, personal representatives, or assigns, in fee simple absolute, clear of all encumbrances, except as set out herein, by a good and sufficient warranty deed, that parcel of land situated in the City of ____________, State of ____________, known as:

________________________________**(zip code**_______**)**

1. The Second Party herein covenants and agrees to pay to the First Party the sum of ________________________________ **($** _______ **.00),** in the following manner:

     a. ____________________Dollars (**$** _______ **.00**) paid to the First Party. Down payment is to be made out to ____________________________.

     b. The principal sum of ________________________________
     (**$** __________ **.00**), with interest thereon at the rate of _______% percent per annum, in monthly installments of
     ________________________________(**$** __________**), beginning on the**
     1ˢᵗ **day of** __________, 20______, and continuing on the 1ˢᵗ day of each and every month thereafter, until Paid in full or until all principal has been paid in full or until termination of this agreement, as provided hereinafter, whichever shall occur first. Payments are considered late after the 5ᵗʰ of the month and will incur a 10% late fee. ALL Monthly Payments are to be made out to

     ____

2. Conveyance shall be by a special warranty deed. The second party will not receive any tax documents from the first party and shall rely solely on the amortization schedule for tax purposes. The First Party grants the right of possession and occupancy to the Second Party upon acceptance of this agreement.

3. Title shall be conveyed free and clear of all encumbrances except, any easements, restrictions, limitations, reservations, covenants and conditions of record not coupled with a possibility of reverter, right of reentry or other reverter right which amounts to a qualification of the fee, and subject also to applicable zoning ordinances and real estate taxes for the year in which the deed is delivered, and

1 of 6   Initials

As you can see, we're basically just entering the buyers' names, the property address, the total price they're paying for it, the down payment amount, and the amount that will be financed. There's a space for the interest rate, the monthly payment amount, and where they'll send payments. That's our first form. See, simple!

This second form, below, says that the second party (buyer) agrees to pay all increases in property taxes. I pay the property taxes on my slow flips, and I recommend that you do too. You could have the buyers pay these taxes, but some won't do it, and you will not find this out for two, three, or four years. By then, you have a hefty bill and a big problem. This form isn't about the general tax bill but any *increases* in property taxes. The truth is, I have never charged my buyers for a property tax increase, but I keep this stipulation in the paperwork just in case taxes suddenly go from $600 a year to $6,000. That's never happened for me, and I don't think it will, but I don't want to be stuck paying that amount in case there's some dramatic rise.

4. The Second Party agrees to pay any and all <u>increases</u> in all property taxes, insurance, assessments, or impositions that may be legally levied or imposed upon said land apportioned as of the date of this Agreement. The current amount of property tax and insurance included in the initial payment amount. The First Party will provide a written notice of any increases as they become due.

This next form is important. It states that the second party may prepay the full principal balance at any time, without penalty and without notice. So, they can pay off the whole loan, the full principal without paying a fee or telling you they're going to do it in advance. However, partial prepayments must be mutually agreed on.

7. **The Second Party** may prepay the FULL principal balance outstanding at any time without penalty and without notice. Such prepayment shall not include unearned interest. Upon full prepayment, the First Party shall have twenty (20) days in which to deliver a warranty deed. **NO PARTIAL PRE-PAYMENTS UNLESS MUTUALLY AGREED UPON.**

The reason for this—and I explain it to buyers in exactly this way—is that if you have a mortgage, I understand that it can really help you to send in an extra $100 or $200 a month. It goes directly to the principal, so it has an outsized financial benefit long-term and can cut your mortgage down from 30 years. For instance, if you make one extra payment a year, it will cut a mortgage down from 30 years to 21 years.

That's huge, right? Great, only I'm not a bank, and I don't have the software of a bank, so if you send me an extra $100, it's just going toward next month's payment. The math gets complicated on an amortization schedule, and I can't be figuring out how an extra $50 this month and $175 next month is affecting it. I tell buyers that if they have an extra $100 a month, or whatever, stick it in the bank. When it gets up to $5,000 or some substantial amount, let me know. You can send it in, and we'll re-amortize the balance then. People usually understand this because it makes the math and the benefit of prepaying easier for them to track too.

The next page we have is just legal language, nothing to worry about, but I do want to mention the rental insurance part of it. My current contract makes buyers responsible for homeowners insurance. I include the name and number of the company they have to call to get a policy. They must include me as an additional insured same as they would any traditional lender. If the house burns down, the insurance payout would be held in escrow, and I would also have to sign checks. Buyers have a choice then. They can opt to rebuild, in which case, the insurance money would be paid directly to a contractor for construction costs, or they can say, there's a payout of $80,000, and I only owe Scott $35,000, so I'll pay him off and keep the difference. Listing the seller on the policy as "additional insured" gives you some control and prevents a buyer from collecting a check for $80,000 or $100,000 and skipping town.

It took me a while to find a company that would insure our buyers as homeowners. The company I use is probably in a dozen states, but they're not everywhere. It might take a minute to find one that works for you, and you want to do this in advance, not after you've sold a house. Since we have significant equity in the house, we also take out a separate insurance policy. Even though we're selling the house, we take out a landlord policy because, technically, we still own it. The buyer is only starting the long process of paying it off and becoming the owner.

If investors buy the house, they will get a landlord policy, which is cheaper than a homeowner's policy. It's also better for us because in that case, we don't need a separate policy. Their tenants would be the ones to get a separate renters policy. Renters insurance is cheap—maybe $100 a year from GEICO—and usually required of all tenants.

I don't force the buyers to require renter's insurance of their tenants, but I encourage it. Most house problems are caused by tenants, so it makes sense. I've only had a few fires at properties over three decades, and every one of them started the same way: a tenant put food on the stove, then went, and took a nap. It's bizarre to me. *"Just stuck this lasagna in the oven, think I'll catch a little shuteye ..."* who sleeps while cooking? More people than you'd think, apparently, but a renter's policy will cover stuff like this. But the landlord doesn't have to require it, and as long as they have their own policy, I'm covered.

This next form we call a compliance sheet. I used to call it a "dummy letter," but I was informed that this wasn't politically correct.

Please Initial and Return

Customer Name____

Property Address____

Because all properties are conveyed by Someday Properties LLC are done so in As-IS condition, we advise you to review the following in an effort to assist you in completing your due diligence prior to finalizing your agreement.

- As an informed buyer you understand that you are responsible from this moment forward that ANY repairs that may be needed will be at your expense.
- INITIAL___________/______________ Date__________

- As an informed buyer you agree that you have inspected the property to your satisfaction and after doing so are comfortable moving forward with all know defects.
- INITIAL___________/______________ Date__________
- As an informed buyer you understand that any payment arrangements that have been made must be kept or you will be considered in default.
  INITIALS__________/______________ Date_______________

- As an informed buyer you understand that all payments are due on the first of the month and will incur a 10% late fee after the fifth of the month. If payment is not received by the 12th, We will have to file an unlawful detainer and you will be responsible for all court costs as well as a $95.00 administration fee.
- INITIALS__________/______________ Date_________________

- As an informed buyer you understand that the seller has done NO inspections and has no knowledge of the condition of the house including but not limited to Plumbing, Hvac, Electrical, Roof ETC. And that any work needed will be solely at the buyer's expense.
- INITIALS__________/____________ Date_________________

This might seem redundant since all of the information on this form is in the paperwork. I created an additional sheet because we're sometimes dealing with first-time buyers or people who suffer from convenient amnesia. They've already heard all of this info, but here, they have to initial next to each item individually. Over the years, I would do all the paperwork with buyers, explain everything in detail to them, and then, a week, three weeks, or three months later, they call and tell me the sink is leaking.

"Were you trying to call a plumber?" I ask. "If so, you accidentally dialed my number."

"But you never told me I had to fix leaks."

Yes, of course, I did, but no matter how clear I made it, someone would always claim not to know that they were responsible for repairs. After this happened a few times, I began making them write their initials next to these items individually. This sheet says in plain language that the buyers understand that they're responsible from this moment forward for any repairs and maintenance. No one can now claim they didn't know.

I want them to state clearly that they have inspected the property and that they are comfortable moving forward with it. They write their initials there so that later, no one can say, I never had a chance to inspect it. I want them to indicate that any payment arrangements they've made must be kept, or they will be in default. I want them to acknowledge that they know there's a 10 percent late fee after five days and that if they don't pay then, they immediately get a five-day notice. If rent is due on the first, and they don't pay, they should know, we'll be filing for eviction after the 12th, as soon as possible (that includes the five days to a late fee, the five days from delivery of the notice, and the weekend that will be included somewhere in there). I'm very strict with that. Do your people a favor by being strict with payment too. You might think you're helping them, but you're actually screwing them by being amicable and passive. It's much easier when you're strict, for them to come up with $900 than when you let things slide month after month, and then they have to come up with $6,000. Trust me, you're helping them by sticking to the rules here.

I charge a $95 administrative fee, as indicated in the paperwork. This defrays my costs if I have to do a court filing. Buyers acknowledge that they understand we have done no inspections and have no knowledge of the condition of the house. This is key. You do not want someone later claiming that you knew there were no pipes under the floorboards. No, I didn't know that. I didn't even see the house. I don't know anything about it, and we're saying so here, in black and white. Their initials show we've been honest about this.

This dummy sheet—sorry, compliance sheet—is not a legal document in the sense that I had a lawyer draw it up, but it comes in handy. I'll give you an example of a time when it earned its keep forever. This woman who was in the military bought a house from us. She was a homeowner living in the property and making monthly mortgage payments to us in an owner-financed deal.

She had some maintenance and repair issues with the house after a time and claimed that she didn't know she was responsible for them. I reminded her that she was. As someone in the military, this buyer had access to free legal counsel. A military lawyer called me up, with this woman sitting in her office. The lawyer got aggressive immediately, saying, her client didn't know she was responsible for repairs, and I never informed her that she was. She read *the Riot Act* to me, half-yelling when I stopped her. I asked if she had a fax machine. That's how long ago this was.

I faxed her the compliance sheet while we were on the phone. The yelling stopped. Then I could hear the lawyer asking her client, "Did you sign this?" The yelling started again but this time, directed at the buyer. "How..." the lawyer asked, "can you claim you didn't know this when your signature is right here?" The lawyer got back on with me and apologized. "Sorry for the inconvenience," she said, "have a nice day." And that was the end of it. I never heard from the buyer or her lawyer again.

My buyer was clearly lying, acting as if she didn't know the terms. It's a stretch to claim ignorance of what's spelled out in an agreement you signed, but when you're initialing things item by item—*"Yes, I understand I am responsible for all repairs; yes, I had a chance to inspect the house..."*—the responsibility is impossible to deny. As I said, this isn't a legal document, but I love it because it clarifies everything. I've had cause to use it a bunch of times, and it has helped defuse some difficult situations.

I go out of my way not to hide anything in doing deals; that only comes back to bite you in the posterior. I live my life and run my business trying to be brutally honest. I want everyone to know everything. A simple sheet like this can help in that effort by making it difficult for anyone to claim later that you lied or hid something.

Receiving Payment

I've said that with slow flipping, your main job becomes cashing checks. That's true, but "collecting payment" might be a better term, since a surprising number of buyers might at times want to pay you in cash.

I used to accept cash from buyers. Around 2001, though, I had a revelation. It was around the fifth of the month when buyers and tenants came in to pay. In addition to investing in real estate, I had a limousine company back then and a small office, with a receptionist at the front desk. In this particular month, I went up front and realized that she had a stack of maybe $50,000 in cash just sitting there. It hit me like a ton of bricks. "I'm going to get robbed! Banks get robbed for $2,000," I thought, and we have tens of thousands in cash sitting here. We don't have cameras, and we have no security.

That was the last day I accepted cash. We put up a sign saying, "No cash accepted" the next morning. The receptionist started turning people away. She told them they'd have to go to 7-Eleven or currency exchange and get us a money order. Dealing with all the money orders became a hassle, so we started using a couple of tech solutions. We used to use www.paynearme.com, and now, we use a similar company called www.aptexx.com. This is a really flexible app that allows your buyers to pay in lots of ways whenever and wherever they want, with a credit card, debit card, check, or on the app. Most important, though, it lets them pay with cash, though the bills never grace your palm.

With www.aptexx.com, your buyers can make a cash payment at participating retailers, such as Target. Someone who wants to pay in cash gets a unique barcode sent to his or her phone. They go into Target or another participating store, get the barcode scanned, pay the cash, and instantly get a receipt emailed to them saying that they paid. As the payee, you get an email saying that the buyer at 123 Main Street paid $800, and the money goes right into your bank account.

Now, no one ever has to come to the office to pay, and we don't have to spend time processing and tracking cash payments. It's another example of automation making our lives easier and allowing us to scale the business without hiring employees. Also, as I said earlier, you want to make things easy for your buyers. You want to give them every chance to make those monthly payments, and this convenience helps.

Insuring Your Slow Flips

Once you buy a slow flip house, you'll want to insure it. As I mentioned, we require our buyers to have homeowners insurance, but you'll want a separate policy. There are lots of options here, but I go with what's called "cash value" on my houses. I didn't always do this. I'll explain how my thinking evolved.

I have a lot of property, which means a lot of insurance, and it can get pretty expensive. At some point, I looked at my insurance bill, and it was really getting up there. I thought, "Man, when I was starting, it was like $600 per property, and now, some of them are $1,400 for the year." I wanted to bring the cost down, but comparing various companies, the rates seemed similar.

Then I realized it all depends on what you ask for. An option called "cash value" allows you to choose the amount you want to insure the house for. I discovered that if I went with cash value, I could insure my typical $30,000 properties for $60,000. If you don't ask for this, the default option is what's called "replacement value." This is exactly what it sounds like. The company looks at a house and says, "Okay, you might have paid $30,000 for it, but it will cost $160,000 to replace, meaning to build a new one like it from scratch." If you don't ask for cash value, they'll charge you insurance rates based on a $160,000 replacement cost.

The upside of choosing replacement value is that if your house were to burn to the ground, you collect $160,000, and you're obviously better off. However, the odds that such a fire will occur are extremely slim. It's likely you'll pay for insurance premiums forever and never even use it. Replacement value might mean an extra $1,000 or so per year. If you want that added comfort, that's fine. The extra dough probably won't break you. Personally, I did the math, and thought, "I'm paying an extra $56,000 or $80,000 a year in total, and I'm going years and years without making claims. As a rule, I would not make a claim unless something catastrophic happened." I figured I can just keep this money, and if something happens, I'll use the savings to do whatever I need to do.

It's not as if I'm leaving myself exposed. I insure all my properties, but I use the cash value option and, generally, double up. If I buy a house for $30,000, I insure it for $60,000. If it burns to the ground, sure, I'd rather get $160,000, but I'll be pretty happy with double my initial investment, and I'll still have the lot to sell. But it probably won't burn down, and I'll save significant money each year. Your insurance agent would rather you take out a policy based on replacement cost, just so you know. It's easier for them to do, and they make more money off it.

They might try to talk you into that option but stick to your guns if you prefer cash value. It's your decision to make.

I've only had maybe four fires, none of them catastrophic, over 30 years, and of the hundreds of houses. One occurred in a small slow flip house. We paid $25,000 for it and had a buyer living there. They did what everyone who starts a fire does—put food on the stove and took a nap. It was just a grease fire in the kitchen and never spread, but it did fill the house with smoke. The walls were black, and everything reeked, but the only actual burning was in the kitchen, where the cabinets were charred.

The person from my insurance company came out to look at the damage and wrote me a check for $25,000. That was, coincidentally, what I'd paid for the house. The payout was based on their estimate of what it would take to repair the damage, not on my purchase price, but the amounts happened to be the same. I did not want to get into rehabbing, so I kept the $25,000, and I sold the place to an investor as is. I made the deal really cheap for him. My first buyer, the person who started the grease fire, had bought the house for $89,000. I sold it to the second investor-buyer for, I think, about $55,000. He went in and completely remodeled it. The deal was owner-financed; of course, another slow flip, and the second buyer paid me $399 a month. Sure, that's low, but it adds up to around $143,000 over 30 years.

The way I saw it, I got the house for free (I paid $25,000, got $25,000 from insurance, and still held the property). I didn't want to rehab it, and I was a little ahead of the down payment and monthly mortgage installments the first buyer paid me. I was happy to collect $399 a month for the next 30 years, and the second buyer did a full rehab of the property to rent it out. I saw it as a win all around. The deal worked for me, and it worked for him.

This house with the grease fire is one example of a cash value scenario where I made a claim, but it's an extremely rare occurrence. The odds are, it will never happen for you, so I think cash value is the way to go on slow flips. That's not true of nicer houses or the house you live in, but for slow flips, it has saved me thousands, maybe hundreds of thousands of dollars over the years. Even if I had to put money into a place because of something catastrophic down the road, it would still be well worth it.

Getting Reviews

We've mentioned your credibility and how important it is in filling your slow flips. Credibility is difficult to establish when you're starting and don't have a track record. Like having a website, creating a Google Business Profile and getting Google reviews are essential to building it. For better or worse, this is the world we live in. The first thing people will check before they do business with you is your online presence, including your Google Business Profile and Google reviews.

Why? Well, for starters, they want to make sure you're legit and just plain real. There have never been more scams and phantoms than in the Internet age, so many, in fact, that we have a term for the con artist who creates a fake persona these days, "the catfish." Buyers want to make sure you're not a catfish. Creating a Google Business Profile is an important step, and it's free.

To create a Profile, go to www.Google.com/business/ and click on "Manage now." Follow the prompts to enter your business name, type of commerce, business category, address, and other details. You can add a description, photos, a logo, and contact info. If you want to dig in, you can post regular updates and current deals. Your Profile will appear on Google Search and Maps as you created it, so you're putting your best foot forward when potential buyers google you.

The best thing about having a Google Business Profile is that you can now start getting reviews. Those reviews will show up next to your Profile in Maps and Search, and prospective buyers will find them immensely useful and comforting. I help my students build profiles and get reviews gradually because it's so important.

I have more than 100 Google reviews, and as I write this, I believe I have 106 five-star reviews (you can check them out online to get an idea of how these go). That's more five-star reviews than any real estate investor in my market. It might seem trivial, but it's actually a powerful tool for my business. When I go on appointments to buy houses, people often say, "Well, I have another offer or someone is coming to make me an offer soon." My response is always the same, "Okay, make sure you check them out and read their reviews. I have more five-star reviews than any other company in all of Hampton Roads (my immediate market in Virginia)." I love being able to say that, and I can because it's true. And buyers love hearing it. They'll sometimes do an online search while I'm there, and I can see the looks of relief and approval on their faces as they scan glowing reviews. It makes them comfortable and happy to see that 100-plus people were here before them and had great experiences. They can read the comments of people saying over and over, "*Yep, we like them ... they were professional, quick and easy to deal with ... here's how our experience went ...*"

Whenever I'm filling properties or have a new landlord I'm working with, I like to be there at the property. They'll say something like, "Well, how do I know this is real?" or "How do I know you're legit?" You're just a guy with some papers and promises. I say, "Well, feel free to google my company. Check us out. Read the reviews." They do, and consistently, they love it. Their comfort level instantly rises.

That's great for you, Scott, after 30 years in the business, some readers are thinking, but I haven't done a single slow flip yet. I don't have any reviews or a way to get them right now. Let me give you two tips for building reviews.

First, if you're brand new like you started today and you've never closed property of any kind, don't lie. You can never fake a review. It will come out later—nothing stays hidden for long online—and that will be worse than having bad reviews. But I tell my coaching partners, "If you don't really have customers yet, or even a business to speak of, you can—without lying—get people to review you." Someone who has never bought or sold a house with you can say, "I've known Scott for 10 years, and he's been honest and trustworthy. I would recommend doing business with him." There's a review. It's quite positive. It will offer a buyer comfort, and it is not a lie. No one is saying they bought or sold a house, just that you're honest. This reviewer is reviewing you as a person. For your first few reviews, until you get the ball rolling, you can take this approach.

The second thing you can do to keep the ball rolling is to incentivize reviews. Let's say you're dealing with someone—you bought a house, sold a house, gave someone a referral, whatever. Of course, you want to say, "Hey, would you mind going on Google and leaving me a review?"

They'll reply, "Oh, absolutely, no problem." Then what? Nothing. Don't take it, personally. We've all been on the other end of this equation. It is human nature. People are busy. They forget; they put it off. It won't get done. Our simple solution to this age-old problem is that when we're sitting across the desk, at the house, at Starbucks, or wherever, I say, "Oh, before I forget, my company is having a promotion right now. We have a $10 Chick-fil-A gift card for you if you leave a review for us on Google. Totally free."

To get the gift card, they have to pull out their phone right then, while they're with us, leave the review and show it to me. Then I give them the gift card. It takes 90 seconds, and virtually everyone will do it. It doesn't matter if your buyer is purchasing a first home to live in or is an investor with $50 million in real estate, they'll all take that gift card. And if you don't get it done then, you'll never see that positive review, despite the best of intentions. Now, we are not steering the review. We're not paying for it, and we're not saying it has to be positive. We have a promotion. People who leave reviews get gift cards. You can't pay for reviews, and you can't coax good ones out of people, but this is allowed, and it works.

It's important to encourage reviews because otherwise, you'll get none or only bad ones. This, too, is human nature, and you've probably been on the flip side of this phenomenon. You might have 20 fantastic meals out at restaurants, and it either doesn't occur to you to leave a nice review online or you think of doing it and don't follow through. You have one rude server and one cold, overpriced dinner and you can't wait to get home to your laptop—at least some people can't. They'll stay up all night carefully crafting sentences for the negative review, but no one can spare two minutes for a positive one.

The lesson is that you have to make it happen, but not in any underhanded or coercive way. As I said, "Never lie. Never pay for a review, but follow our commonsense steps." And you'll begin to amass a track record in this important virtual arena. It's also nice, by the way, to comment on positive Google reviews as they start to come in. When Claudia says, "What a dreamboat you were to work with," click on her review to reply, "Thanks, Claudia, so great to work with you, too!" or whatever.

A Google Business Profile and positive reviews are key to establishing credibility. So is a key, a great big one, as in the photo below.

As you might have guessed, that's my smiling customer with the giant key, taking possession of a house after the paperwork was signed. I always take pictures of my buyers when they come in and approve our agreements (note that I didn't say "sign contracts"). Sometimes, we do it at the house, which is nice for the photo, and sometimes at the office. We take pictures either way. I bought this giant key off eBay or somewhere online for $50. Google "giant key cut out" or something like that, and you'll see options.

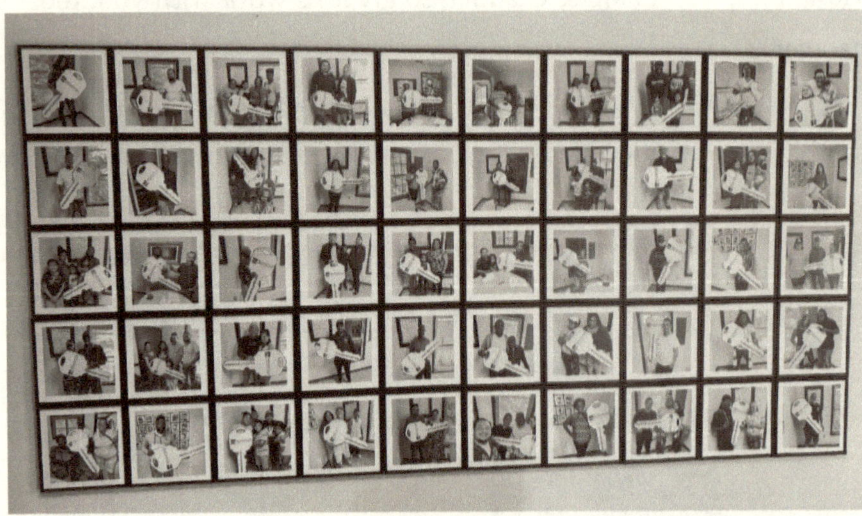

I started doing this a few years ago, but I wish I'd started it 15 years ago so that I'd have hundreds and hundreds of such photos. I print them out and post them on the walls of the room where people come to do paperwork.

This might seem cheesy or smack of the Publishers Clearinghouse Sweepstakes, but it's real, and it works. When people sit down in that office and look up to see that 30 or 40 other people sat here before them and happily completed the process, they get comfortable and confident.

No one wants to be the first. It's one thing to tell someone you've had hundreds of satisfied customers. Anyone can say that. Here, people can see those customers, smiling and holding a symbolic key on the day they took possession of the houses they bought from me. Buyers know they haven't stepped into some elaborate con or internet scam, and they can turn their money over without worrying. In addition to the office walls, we post these pics on our Advantage Homebuyers Google page and on our Facebook page to promote our brand. The giant key is a great marketing tool that costs about $50, and you can use it repeatedly.

You now have a good handle on the formula for slow flipping as I do it and why it's the fastest possible path to wealth. We've also explored in depth how to find, market, and close slow flips, but we saved a very important piece of the puzzle for last—financing. We don't use banks or institutional lenders on slow flips, but private lenders who want a better return on their money than they're getting from savings accounts, stocks, or bonds. What is "private money?" Where does it come from and how can you raise it? We'll explore this topic in depth in Chapter 6.

6

Raising Private Money

In this chapter, we'll dig into financing your slow flips. Up to now, we've talked about funding your slow flips with "private money," but only defined that term in brief. Private money is just what it sounds like—private funds held by normal people who want a better return on their cash than they can get from the usual investment vehicles. It's all around you, as you'll discover once you learn to look for it.

Why not use a bank to finance your slow flips—a process many readers are familiar with from buying their own homes? As you probably know, getting loans from banks or other conventional lenders is cumbersome and difficult. You need a good credit score. They will examine your gross income for the last several years and your monthly expenses. They'll want to see bank statements. And to buy a house with a bank loan, you need a cash down payment. The process can be time-consuming too, which means your deal would likely disappear by the time the loan got approved—if it got approved. Typical bank loans for homes also have 30-year terms, which as you now know, means you're signing on to work for Mr. Burns for the next three decades. Since our goal in a slow flip is to pay off our loans in five years (buy it like a car, sell it like a house), a 30-year or even 15-year mortgage won't work.

When you use private money, there are no credit checks or bank statements and no bureaucratic hoops to jump through. You can access the money quickly, borrowing it and paying it back on your terms. You call the shots with private money because you're establishing a program for lenders. If you approach the process in the right way, with the right mindset and presentation, your lenders or investors will see your offer as a coveted opportunity, not as a favor or even as a "loan." In the coming pages, I'll show you how to establish your program for private-money lenders and how to identify and approach them. We'll explore how to put your program out there, build relationships, develop an elevator pitch, and create a brag book.

Many readers will start this chapter feeling shy or unconfident about cultivating private money. By the end of it, however, you will have the tools and methods to keep you from ever getting rejected. Just as we've seen in real estate, that transition involves a change in mindset. *"That credit card company isn't offering to "approve" you but to "enslave" you... That mess in the house isn't a problem; it's lucky for you. Let me explain why ... Leaving some money for the next guy is a good thing ... Celebrate his success!"* You don't need to be a genius to make money as a real estate investor, but you do need to think about things from the right perspective and in the right context. Private money is a prime example, as you'll soon see.

Hard Money

Before we explore private money, I want to briefly mention "hard money" because people often confuse the two. I have used hard money for various deals over the years, and rehabbers frequently use it to fund renovations and flip properties. Those are fast, or conventional, flips, though. We do not want to use hard money for slow flips.

Hard money loans are short-term loans, or "bridge" loans, with high-interest rates secured by real property. These loans are relatively easy to get because the borrower doesn't qualify; the house qualifies, which is also true of private money. If you pay off your hard-money loans, the lenders earn great returns from the high-interest rates they charge. If you default, the lender takes the house, which is an even better deal for them. A borrower can generally close on one of these loans in as little as a week. Hard money is expensive to borrow but worth it for rehabbers, because it allows them to scale quickly, without using their own money or jumping through bureaucratic hoops, and they're banking on quick turnover anyway.

The big difference between a hard-money lender and a private lender—I want to make sure you understand this—is that hard-money lenders are in the business of lending money. They are professionals who make their living lending funds. This means that they call the shots every time. You don't decide on an interest rate or terms; they do. If you don't like their offer, move along. They have plenty of takers, and they're not going to change their program for you. Most hard money loans are short-term, six months max. This fits the window of a typical rehabber, who hopes to get a house renovated, marketed, and sold within that timeframe. It does not work for a slow flip, where we want to pay off our loans in five years.

As slow flippers, we want to control our own program, not adhere to some lender's program. Using private money puts us in control, as we'll see. We're the ones calling the shots and setting terms, telling private lenders that if you don't like them, they can move along. We can learn some lessons from hard-money lenders, though. They have established rules, an agenda, or a set program, and they stick to it. We want to do the same thing in dealing with private money lenders. Hard-money lenders are also happy to see others profit. They don't look at their returns and think, "That rehabber just cleared eighty grand using my loan, and I only made $1,100." They focus on their own very high rates and great returns, and they're glad when clients do well because it means the lender is getting paid and will likely get paid again when this customer returns.

One final note on hard-money lenders! Since some readers might use them for other types of investing down the road. They are in business to make money, obviously, and as I mentioned, they qualify the deal, not the borrower. If they turn you down for a loan, they've deemed that the deal in question is a bad one. They tend to know what they're doing, so if you get turned down by a hard-money lender, don't search for a new lender; search for a new deal.

Private Money

As I said above, private-money lenders are normal people who want a better return on their cash than they can get from typical investment vehicles. They are not professional lenders. What does "normal" mean? Well, there are lots of folks out there who have $50,000, $100,000, or $300,000 in retirement money, savings, bank accounts, or just sitting under the mattress. I'm talking about your mailman, your dentist, the owner of the corner restaurant, or a patron you chat with there. Your cousin Phil or Aunt Margaret's second husband or that grease-monkey buddy from high school who opened his own autobody shop and made bank.

As you start to think about it and look around, you'll be surprised at how much cash some people have on hand. They're earning 3 percent or less on it in savings or maybe in the 5 percent range with a good annuity. Sometimes, the money has been sitting in a check or a shoebox and earning nothing. If they buy stocks, they've probably had good months and terrible months, but the only thing they can count on in the market is volatility and the anxiety that comes with it.

Put yourself in the shoes of these normal Joes, with cash sitting around, earning little to no return as retirement looms. Or maybe retirement has already arrived, and they're now on fixed incomes, nervous that they no longer make money, but must live on a steady nut. The notion of earning a 10 or 12 percent return over five years, from an investment backed by real property looks pretty appealing, doesn't it?

These lenders are similar to hard-money lenders in the sense that there is no bank involved. There is no corporate structure to deal with, no credit checks, bank statements, or analysis of monthly expenses. With both hard money and private money, the bureaucratic hoops are eliminated because the deal is getting qualified, not the borrower. The biggest difference, as I mentioned, is that a private money lender is a regular person who is not in the business but has funds available and would like to earn more money. This means you are the one creating the program and soliciting those funds. You make an offer: here's the chance to make X percent over Y years. And you set the terms.

How do you build a program and set those terms?

Building a Program

You already know how long you want your typical private-money loan for—five years. In the slow flip model, which you're now familiar with, we buy houses as if they're cars—on five-year loans. This differs from a bank loan, which usually has a 30-year or sometimes, a 15-year term, as we said, and from a hard-money loan, which is usually for a maximum of six months. The timeframe is up to you, as are interest rates and other terms. You decide—based on your investments and comfort level—what fits your ideal slow flip scenario. The box is yours to make, and the private-money lenders can decide if it's one they want in on or not.

I recommend a five-year term because the whole point of a slow flip is to get out of debt and have a house free and clear as quickly as possible. If, however, you decide for some reason that a shorter term or slightly longer term works for you, you can establish that parameter. As you know, I pay my private lenders 12 percent. That's a number that works well for me. It ensures that I always have money available and that my lenders do well on my deals. But if that sounds exorbitant, you can start with a rate of 10 percent, 8 percent, or even 6 percent—whatever you want to try—and see how it goes. I went high right out of the gate because when I started doing slow flips in 2011, there was an abundance of properties on the market. I wanted to make sure I had an abundance of lenders to facilitate buying as many of them as I could, and a rate of 12 percent guaranteed that I got them. My plan was that once I had more money available, more properties, and a track record with these private lenders, I would then go back and lower the rate I paid, but I never did.

One reason I didn't come down from 12 percent is that I don't actually pay it, my buyers do. Thinking of it this way made the rate almost a non-issue for me. The house was essentially free to me, so I wasn't too worried about my interest rate. I have many more lenders now, but those first lenders referred the others to me. If I was going to remain consistent with the first group, I didn't want to say to the rest, "Okay, the friend who referred you is making 12 percent, but I'm paying you 8 percent." I wanted to make the same offer to everyone. That's just my take. You need to decide on your own rates when raising private money and starting out. You might want to try a lower one. You can adjust it up or down later with new lenders.

As you think about developing your program for private lenders and the interest rate you'll pay, test your numbers on one of the many free amortization calculators available online. On a $30,000 loan—pretty small, as home loans go—the difference between the high-interest rate I'm paying and one that sounds more reasonable might be smaller than you imagine. My $30,000 loan from a private money lender at 12 percent gives me a $667 monthly payment. If I lower the interest rate I'm paying to 9 percent, my payment is around $622, just $45 less per month. My lenders are thrilled to get 12 percent because that's an enormous guaranteed rate of return. This is the number they're fixated on, and when it hits 12, their eyes pop. Where else can you get that kind of payback, with virtually no risk? A return of 9 percent is still healthy, but it's more likely to get a quiet thumbs-up than a "wow!" I want the "wow" from my lenders to keep the money freely flowing and for $45 a month—paid by my buyer, not me—it's well worth the higher rate.

It helps your model to have private-money lenders who are not just willing but excited and eager to work with you. All of my lenders love dealing with me. In fact, I've only had one ever turn me down. This was a big-money guy, with very deep pockets. One of my other lenders referred him to me, and I was excited to meet him for lunch. This, I thought, is the big leagues. We met, and I gave him a standard spiel—$30,000 loans with five-year terms, paying 12 percent interest. He said he would think about it.

He thought about it and then, a week or two later, turned me down. I found his reason funny, but it wasn't something I could argue with. "This is too good to be true," he said. "Nobody can pay 12 percent." "That was it. Something must be fishy here," he thought. Because this is too good a deal. I didn't argue, of course. I never try to convince anybody of anything, though he almost seemed like he wanted me to talk him into the idea. He kept saying, "You know if something seems too good to be true, it probably is." And this seems just too good to be true. The friend who referred this guy to me started showing him statements each year when he did his taxes. Look, I made $86,000 in interest last year from Scott's program. I made $82,000 in interest from Scott. He realized eventually that the deal was real, but seven or eight years on, he felt it was too late to jump in. At that point, the return might just have highlighted for him all the money he missed out on over the years because of his initial caution. The irony is that if I'd offered him 5 percent, he probably would have jumped at it.

Rates and monthly payments for a 5-year $30,000 loan

Interest Rate	Monthly Payment
12	$667
11	$652
10	$637
9	$622
8	$608
7	$594
6	$579

Finding Private Money

Having private lenders will lead to more private lenders, but how do you get that first group? Where do you begin looking for private money?

Start, enthusiastically, with friends and family. I work closely with many students, coaching them on investment strategies, and when I say this early on, they scoff. "That's fine for you," they say, "but I don't have any friends or family with money." "I don't know anyone who could invest at this level. I don't move in those sorts of circles."

Yes, you do. We all do. Discretionary dollars exist in everybody's circle. Those same students who tell me they don't know a soul with money, but follow my strategy, soon return, saying, "Yep, I have money lined up for all the deals I want to do." Now, it might be a fact that not one person in your immediate family or group of friends has a spare nickel. That's rare, believe it or not. When people think this, it usually means they are simply unaware of money sitting within arm's reach. Did you approach Uncle Jack who lives so frugally with an opportunity that he can't really refuse? Guess what? He grew up during the Depression and because he was so frugal, he will leave a bank account that shocks you. The guy driving the beater, the lady who gets two channels because she refuses to pay for cable, or the people dressed like they might be homeless—they often have more money than you would ever guess, and they're often shrewd about managing it. This is why they have it and why your program will appeal to them.

But let's not get ahead of ourselves. Even if all your immediate friends and family together couldn't pool enough dough for a sandwich, we start with them. We're not hitting them up for loans—we don't hit anyone up for a loan—we're simply putting the word out. We're telling them what we do. *"I'm investing in real estate these days, and here's how it works... I've started buying houses as investment properties, with a system that offers great returns ... I'm really excited about this new investing I'm doing because..."*

We tell anyone and everyone we talk to, starting with friends and family, about this exciting new thing we're doing. This is networking that's easy to do and can reap amazing results.

I don't wear my "We Buy Houses" shirts for fun. I always have one on, with that message plastered across the back if it's a tee shirt and on the front if it's a polo. Over the years, I've seen how effective it can be. Hardly an hour, much less a day, goes by that someone doesn't notice the shirt. They ask, "What's that about? What sort of houses do you buy? Why? What do you do with them?" Sometimes, they have a house they want to sell quickly, or they know someone who does, or they will know someone who does in three months, a year, or two years from now. They'll remember then, "Oh, Scott buys houses." "Maybe you should call this "We Buy Houses" guy I know." When I mention that ordinary people finance my investments, not banks, people pretty much always want to know how those investments payout. Many are intrigued by the answer.

I am the "We Buy Houses" guy, and everybody knows that. Lest you doubt my commitment, check out the photo below.

That's right, even my shoes advertise the fact that I buy houses. Okay, I don't wear those every day, but I do own them. The point is I am putting it out there constantly that I buy houses. I invest in real estate. This is what I do. It's a major part of my life, and I want to make sure that everyone knows about it. You need to put the word out there that you are buying houses as part of an exciting real estate investment business. Start with your friends and family because (a.) You're around them and comfortable with them, so those are easy conversations to have and in which to practice explaining what you do and (b.) Even if no one in that immediate circle has money to invest, many of them will know someone who does.

This is how networks are built. When Cousin Sue hears from her kid's orthodontist that he and some colleagues invested spare money in an apartment building that has turned into a headache, it will jog her memory. "Oh, yeah?" "My cousin is doing something like that, buying up houses as investments, but he's really excited about it. He says, the way he's doing it, there are no headaches ..."

When your friend Dave's father-in-law complains about a stock market plunge, Dave will remember that you're paying investors a steady 12 percent for something involving real estate and will pique the old man's interest.

Here is another example of the thousand I could give of how to put out the word about what you do. I know a guy who, when he started raising money for deals, would go to coffee shops in the nicest part of town to work. Like half the people hanging out in coffee shops these days, he made his business calls there, and during lulls, he called friends to talk over his deals. Everyone in the room heard how he was investing in real estate and paying his private lenders a steady 12 percent return, risk-free since the loans were secured with property worth far more than the amount invested. "The investors can't lose," he would say, casually, debriefing a friend. "They're banging down my door to get into more deals. That's the easy part. I can't keep up on the buying side because they always want to know when the next deal's coming ..."

Every time my friend did that, someone struck up a conversation about his business or dropped a card on his table on the way out, saying, "Hey, give me a call about your investing. I'd love to hear more." The idea is to always and in every way possible, put the word out there about what you're doing. I realize that I sound like an Eastern mystic repeating this, but it is another case of real estate karma. What you put out there in the universe will return to you. We're not talking about begging for money or even asking for loans. You're simply spreading the word. This hopefully takes some of the anxiety out of the notion of private money. We are not walking around hat in hand, as my students sometimes imagine when I first mention the idea.

After friends and family, spreading the word among your coworkers is another obvious move. People at the office, factory, restaurant—wherever you work—know you and trust you, and you never know what money they might have squirreled away, looking for a home. Grandparents and aunts die and leave $50,000 or $150,000 to that favorite relative, who's often unsure what to do with it. Meanwhile, it sits in a savings account or even checking, earning little to nothing. There might well be someone among your coworkers looking to make money off a nest egg. The accountant who does your taxes and other professionals you deal with are prime candidates, too. Your CPA understands math and appreciates a good return on investment and, of everyone you know, will understand the dynamics of slow flipping right away.

My very first private lender was a woman who owns a club in my area, not a nightclub, but a private club where businesspeople go to eat lunch and have meetings. I've been a member there since she opened it. I talked to her one day to see if she could set me up with other club members who might be interested in funding my deals for a good return. I honestly had no intention of asking her to be a lender, but it was one of those happy accidents that helped me develop the strategy I'm encouraging in this chapter. I went through the whole process with her and explained my deals and the terms I would offer club members who wanted to become lenders. When I finished, she immediately said, "Well, what about me? Can I do it?" "Of course," I said, "Why not? And she became my very first private lender." Yep, I learned this approach the way I've learned everything—the hard way, which is why I'm trying to streamline the process for others here.

My second lender—similar story—was my attorney. He saw the deals I'd done over the years, and when I started slow flipping, I approached him just as I had approached the club owner. "Hey, I'm trying this new program funded with private money, and I wonder if you know anyone who might be interested." "I'm interested," he said. "How do I get in on this?"

Never Get Rejected

As I hope you're beginning to see, raising private money does not involve asking for loans. We'll expand on the idea of just how to put the word out there and develop your "elevator pitch" in a moment, but first, let me ease another fear. Talking up a blue streak about your real estate investing will not make you a bore. Just the opposite. There's no reason to be shy or embarrassed about this. After a lifetime in real estate, I can tell you, unequivocally, that people are fascinated by it. You are, too, on some level, or you wouldn't still be reading this book. That fascination stems from the fact that real estate is the one business that touches all our lives, all day every day. Whether you rent, own, or live in public housing, you wake up in a piece of property. What it's worth and how it's maintained or managed deeply affect your life. You get in a car or board a bus in the morning and go past endless other properties to get to the office, plant, school, or store, where you work in another piece of real estate that will shape your day. When you go to your friend's birthday party next week, she and her husband will give you a tour of their new place or if it's old, show you how they redid the family room or discuss how they plan to landscape the yard. Another couple will wonder if they should renovate, and a third will complain about how much it now costs to move up to something bigger in the neighborhood, given appreciation and rising interest rates, and so on.

Real estate affects us all, and we all know something about it. You don't have to have a degree or expertise or education to get into it. I am living proof of that, right? I dropped out of high school, got interested in buying houses, and educated myself about real estate bit by bit over the years. The many TV shows now devoted to flipping, rehabs, and home improvement only play on a fascination most people already have. Everyone is intrigued by real estate, and by "everyone," I mean your dentist, doctor, mailman, mechanic, cousin, coworkers, neighbors, and old high school friends ... Many of them are thinking, *I always wanted to get into real estate investing, on the side, if not full-time ... I always thought it would be cool to flip a house or be a landlord ... Seems like there's good money to be made in real estate. I wish that when I was younger ..."*

When people find out that you invest in real estate, they'll be excited, not bored. They'll grill you about the particulars. It's part of your job to inform them about the process, and once you do, some will want in on the action.

You will never be rejected, following my approach, partly because you're never really asking anyone for money or struggling to get a loan. You are putting the word out about an exciting real estate investment program that offers a great return with virtually no risk. The pushiest thing you do is ask your coworkers, cousin, or CPA if they know anyone who might be interested. You're not asking if "they" are interested, but casually presenting an opportunity in case it interests someone in their circle. They might very well know someone and make an introduction, but they're just as likely to say, "What about me?" We are capitalizing, in an extremely low-pressure way, on what the kids today call FOMO—fear of missing out. The last thing your dentist wants is for Jerry down the hall to cash in on this great opportunity before she gets a shot at those 12 percent returns.

Just to be clear: you never ask someone to loan you money. You offer an opportunity, but not to the person you approach. We're letting that person know about our investing because they might know someone who would be interested. And then, we wait for the inevitable response, which is, "Well, why don't you tell me about it, I might be interested." We then downplay the possibility with that person. "Well, I know you're into a bunch of other stuff. You're busy. You have other investments, whatever. I was thinking maybe someone in your law firm or at your office or some of your clients might be interested..." Not only are you not hitting them up, but you're also making them beg to hear more. "No, not at all," they'll say, "I might be interested in something like that." This allows you to maintain your position of power and flip the usual script.

Your approach is a conscious, premeditated version of the one I stumbled onto with my attorney and that club owner years ago. Don't ask for anything. Let them ask, "Would you accept me? Could I be one of the investors earning 12 percent?" This dynamic depends entirely on your mindset. If you go out with hat in hand like a beggar, that's how you'll be treated. You'll be full of fear, and you'll never do it. If you see yourself as a gatekeeper with the coveted key to 12 percent returns, potential lenders will look at you in an entirely different light.

Develop an Elevator Pitch

Once people send potential lenders your way or step up themselves to ask about the opportunity, you need an initial elevator pitch. Every Hollywood movie is born as an "elevator pitch," and that's what gets the ball rolling on business deals too. You must have your program fully developed, with your terms and answers to possible objections fully fleshed out, and then condense it into a 30-second summary of what you do.

The pitch exists to whet appetites. It will pretty much always lead to questions from whoever hears it, but you want to keep it short and sweet and let them do the asking. If you launch into a long explanation right off the bat, it will seem like you're selling something, and that's not the impression you want to give.

Before you can condense your program into an elevator pitch, you need a program. By now, you know my system for slow flips inside and out. I've shared with you my formula and detailed strategies for finding, marketing, and closing slow flips. I buy distressed houses for $30,000, using private money borrowed for five years at 12 percent interest. I sell those houses "as is," with owner-financed 30-year mortgages for $89,000—that's $875 a month, with $3,000–$5,000 down. I recommend this formula because I know it works, but you can vary your program in ways that fit your needs, comfort level, or local market. Whatever parameters you decide on, get your formula down.

A discussion with a potential private lender is not the time to develop your program, but to explain one you've already developed. Your terms should be set because you certainly don't want to let lenders set them. You never ever want to go into a meeting with a lender and say, "Well, what sort of terms do you want? What kind of interest rate would you like to charge me? On what period do you want to be paid back? What would make you happy?" You'll say, "Here is the program. I borrow $30,000 on a 60-month mortgage at 12 percent interest, or maybe it's $50,000 at 6 percent for 5 years." Whatever your formula, get it down and stick to it. The potential private lender either fits into your box or doesn't, but the box is solid and unalterable. Here is what I do. "How about 14 percent?" "Nope." Not a conversation. I make the box, not you.

Don't think to yourself, "Well, it's my first time, and I just need a lender, any lender, so I'll make an exception." Remember, I'm still using my first group of lenders from 2011, and my other lenders all stemmed from that group. You want your lenders for the long term. You want to build relationships with them, as we'll explore shortly, so, it's best to set careful terms early on and be as consistent as possible. A solid program shows you in a more professional light and will make it easier to get lenders.

My most basic elevator pitch when people ask what I do is "I help people place their money in high-performing assets secured by real estate."

"Really? Tell me more about that."

Nearly everyone will respond with some version of "tell me more," and then, you can ease into the details. You explain your program and the opportunities it's creating for private lenders who want to earn 12 percent or whatever you're paying. You're not asking questions, and you're not soliciting.

It's important to have your program fleshed out before you deliver that elevator pitch precisely because more questions will follow. Lots of people promise all sorts of crazy returns, so be prepared for skepticism about that 12 percent (remember the big-money guy who turned me down). Surely, they'll say, "This must be a risky investment to pay that high. Where's the security?"

Your answer is that "My deals are secured by a note in 'deed of trust,' —the same documents that banks have when they loan money for mortgages." For every deal, I provide the same documents that a bank would—a note and deed of trust secured against the property. Understandably, people want to know how they're protected. They ask, "What's my risk? What's the worst that can happen for me in one of these deals?" "My answer is always the same." "The worst thing that can happen is that I pay you perfectly each month and you make 12 percent on the loan."

If that happens, your lender is earning around $10,000 in interest on their $30,000 loan over five years, an incredible return, and that is the "worst" scenario for them. The other possibility is that I default and can't make good on payments for some reason. I get sick, say, or fall into addiction, or disappear after a year. If that happens, the lender takes possession of the property or has a foreclosure auction, and earns significantly more than the agreed interest. Now, they have a house that has probably been renovated and is worth $90,000 or more in return for their $30,000 loan.

Having these scenarios in your back pocket puts you in a strong position. I make sure all my payments go out on the first of the month, and I make sure of this with my coaching clients, too. I impress our reliability and punctuality upon my lenders, but I also tell them that this is actually their downside. The worst thing that can happen is that I pay you on time and you only make the phenomenal 12 percent return we agreed on. If things go badly for me and for some reason, I can't keep paying, that's the upside for my private lenders. In that case, they take possession of a property worth maybe triple the original loan amount.

Underline the passage above or jot it down in your notes. It's one of the most powerful tools you have in attracting private lenders and another reason you won't get rejected.

Building Relationships

As you identify and cultivate private money, I encourage you to focus on trust and relationship building. Banks deal in paper relationships. For them, borrowers exist as lines on a form or entries in a database, and for borrowers, banks are simply big cold institutions, often with headquarters across the country. You never meet Mr. Burns—he's just the anonymous guy cashing your checks in some distant corner office. Your lenders will meet you, get to know you, check in with you, and see how your deals are going. Yes, they'll cash your checks and be happy to do so, but the relationships run much deeper with private money.

This isn't BS or some feel-good pep talk. Sure, it's a nicer way to do business and live your days, dealing with a network of people who know and trust you, but it's more than that. You will count on your lenders over the long haul. As I keep repeating, I have the same private lenders that I've had since 2011, and everyone who came on board later is a branch growing off that original tree. Building these relationships is a lifelong process. Over the years, my lenders have had friends ask, "Do you think Scott would take on another investor?" "I get calls from my people, saying, 'I hope I'm not hurting myself here, but I have a buddy who also wants to get in on these deals and loan you money.'" "Do you have enough to go around?" They ask sheepishly because they don't want to limit their own ability to invest and earn a 12 percent return.

When those friends of lenders come on board, there's immediate trust because I've been working for years with someone they know. "How well do I know them?" My private lenders are friends at this point. They have funded so many deals, over a decade or more in many cases. My family and I have gone on trips to the Bahamas with my private lenders. We went to Jamaica with one of my lenders and his family, and we've gone on casino trips together. Managing people's money and paying them a handsome return, you get to know them really well.

My longtime lenders, who understand the benefits and low-risk profile of slow flipping, also loan to my coaching students. I review the deals for those lenders and make sure the numbers work, which is a pretty high level of trust to put in me and the program. Even if someone only has a limited amount to loan, let's say $100,000 to do three deals at $30,000 each, they'll be back. They'll profit from those deals; the pot will replenish itself, and they'll want to reinvest their earnings by loaning you more. As long as you're paying a steady 12 percent return, they're going to keep coming back. It is yet another case of—you guessed it— real estate karma, and it's worth its weight in gold. I never have to delay a deal because I'm looking for money. The private money is always there, and in fact, I have to spread the love carefully to keep my lenders happy. They're so eager to get in on more deals.

Make a Brag Book

You won't be able to make a "brag book" starting, but assembling photos, details, and videos from your deals as you progress is vital. That's all a brag book is—your track record of successful deals. It's easy to create, given today's technology, but you have to think about this project and work on it as you go. Photographing a property is quick and painless these days. Your phone is more than adequate to get some down-and-dirty shots, but there's no way to go back and get "before" pictures of a house once it's renovated. You have to get your photos and videos and methodically record the details as you go. Make it a standard part of every deal and before long, you'll have an impressive brag book assembled.

Always take before and after pictures of slow flips. Take smiling pictures of the people you sell your houses to, and put willing lenders' information down in your brag book for each deal. You obviously need their permission to do this. Including them is important because potential private-money lenders will want to talk to others who have invested in slow flips to hear how the experience went and what sort of return they realized. If your current lender agrees, put down who funded the deal, for how much, and under what terms. Ideally, the lenders in your brag book will make themselves available to talk to others who are considering loaning you money. This is yet another reason why building trust with your lenders is so critical.

My relationships with my lenders are so good. They actually do this for my coaching students too, to help them raise private money. When I'm coaching, I'll get on a three-way call with my students and potential lenders to explain a slow flip, but sometimes, they would rather talk to another lender who's been involved for a decade than talk to the coach. My lenders let my students' private-money prospects call them as references to discuss how slow flipping works and how their deals have gone.

You obviously can't put videos in a physical book, but you can print URLs for before and after videos that you've put online, alongside the pictures in the book. Be specific about the properties, both in those videos and in the books. Include dates, actual addresses, photos, prices, interest rates, and lenders when possible (always and only with permission!). Remember that some of your private-money lenders might have experience in real estate, but many won't. Your dentist, landscaper, or second cousin might be intrigued, but they'll also need some handholding. Early in *The Art of the Slow Flip*, you might have thought that a $30,000 house either didn't exist or could only mean four sheets of plywood with a tarp on top, and then, you saw in these pages before and after photos of actual slow flips I have done. You've seen that many of these houses need serious cleanup and repairs, but they're also functional, livable homes with potential. Photos detailing the work that our buyers have done—the new granite counters, new hardwood, fresh AC units, new roofs, etc.—are convincing. It's important to show your potential lenders that narrative with before and after pics as you get them.

Having this sort of proof of concept along with our worst-case scenario from above (earning 12 percent is the absolute *worst* that can happen) will guarantee a steady flow of private money so that you're never scrambling to fund deals as they arise.

Private Placement Memorandum (PPM)

We call the loans we get in slow flipping "private money" because they are, by necessity, private. You can't go online or on the radio, for instance, and solicit lenders to become part of an investment pool that you'll use to buy houses. Once you start publicly raising money and mingling funds in that way, you are selling a "security," which works the same way stocks, bonds, and other similar financial instruments do. Securities are subject to the rules and regulations of the Securities and Exchange Commission and get very complicated very quickly.

To legally raise money in this way, you would have to create what's called a private placement memorandum, pay a ton of expenses, and jump through many regulatory hoops. This is the sort of stuff investment bankers spend their days on, and in my opinion, it doesn't make any sense for a small-time individual real estate investor. I tried it once, thinking it would help me to scale, and I hated it. Now, I strictly use one lender for one house. I don't raise money publicly, from solicitations online, or in other media, and I don't mix people's money.

You might see examples of investors out there doing exactly what I'm saying you cannot do, but they're probably skirting the law. They might get away with it, but they're taking a major risk. Don't do it. It's not worth the trouble, and you don't need to raise money in this way if you take the approach we've outlined in this chapter. You are allowed to raise money from anybody you have private conversations with or have any kind of relationship with—a cousin, coworker, or friend of a friend. Make these deals one-on-one and do each slow flip with a single lender's funds. It is fine if one lender wants in on three houses, but my advice is "Don't ever use two lenders on a single house." If during our discussion of raising private money, a light bulb went off, and you thought, "I'll put up some Facebook posts or make videos or do a podcast to raise money, forget it." You could be seen as selling security, and that's not a swamp you want to wade into.

If you are highly organized and financially savvy, and you're determined to raise money in this way, you must pay to set up a private placement memorandum and follow all the regulations. When I tried that route, I spent almost $30,000 to get mine done, and I had a bad experience. There was so much regulation, reporting, and red tape, as well as expense, that I quickly shut it down. I thought to myself, "I am going back to one lender for one house and sticking with that model."

Get Excited!

Raising private money is obviously one of the keys to slow flipping. Without private lenders, the deals can't happen. Feeling some fear or anxiety about cultivating lenders is completely normal. Most of us don't want to go around, hat in hand, asking friends, relatives, coworkers, and the concentric rings of people emanating from that core, for money. I hope that after reading this chapter, you realize that is not all that we do, and that seeing our approach has eliminated or drastically cut down on your fear.

We're not asking for money, simply talking about what we do, an enterprise that people are fascinated by. Get into the right mindset. You're putting the word out there and mentioning opportunities that offer an amazing return—the kind of investment anyone would kill to get on. Get excited about what you're doing, and your enthusiasm will be infectious. As you start talking about slow flipping and the return you can give investors, your confidence will grow. It will swell as you build relationships, practice your elevator pitch, and create a brag book. You don't need to fear rejection ever because we've given you an approach that guarantees you'll never get rejected.

Conclusion

Start Building Wealth Today

As I said at the start of this book, slow flipping is not a get-rich-quick scheme. It requires patience and planning. We're in it for the long haul. If you want quick checks and a fast payoff, you could try flipping the conventional way, "fast flipping." That means buying a house that's the worse for wear (probably with a bank loan), spending considerable time and effort to rehab and clean it up, then marketing it for retail sale. If all goes well, conventional flipping can get you a hefty check within months. It's quite possible that not all will go well. However, you'll probably need good credit or a pile of your own money to flip houses this way. It also helps to know something about construction.

Wholesaling, in which you contract a property, mark it up, then assign the contract to another investor who will rehab and retail it himself, also results in fast checks. It has fewer risks and fewer bureaucratic hoops than conventional flipping, but despite the quick checks, neither of these methods builds real wealth. Remember, by "wealth," I mean passive income—more money coming in than going out steadily, without the need for work unless cashing checks counts as work. The goal with slow flipping isn't a quick check but a deep well of income that endlessly renews itself. Rentals get closer to the slow flip approach because they're a long-term proposition, but as I hope I've made clear, the idea of rentals translates into a reality of endless headaches—toilets to plunge, AC units to replace, or tenants to chase—all for a theoretical payoff 30 years down the road.

Slow flipping requires no rehabbing, no maintenance, and, thankfully, no tenant complaints. As we've seen, compared to rentals or rehabbing, there's very little risk, and you don't have to use your own money. The checks don't come quickly—you'll break even for five years—but once those short-term private-money loans are paid off and income starts streaming in, you are, literally, home-free. Your job, like our hero, Mr. Burns' job, is simply to make deposits at the bank.

Our horizon as slow flippers is just 60 months away. That's when the payoff comes and where freedom lies if you start today. If you spend the next year thinking about the possibilities, browsing, doing research, and making plans, your horizon for freedom and future vision will be six years off. But trust me, it's easy for that year to turn into two, for two to become three, and for that vision to grow ever more distant until retirement is around the corner, or long past, and you still haven't begun investing.

Don't equate long-term with lackadaisical. If anything, the fact that you won't make a profit from slow flipping for five years should create a sense of urgency. My strong recommendation is that you get started now, this week, or today if possible. Obviously, you can't go out and buy a house on day one, but you can plunge into likely markets and start getting a feel for where you want to buy. You can start building a website, getting business cards made, and putting out the word about your exciting new investment opportunity for potential private-money lenders. I currently have a student with 50-plus houses under his belt. He'd never heard of a slow flip before I worked with him, and now, he's killing it just a few years in. I have another student who complains that he can't find any slow flips and that the system doesn't work. They both started in the same position, with zero experience, and they were given the exact same information. The first student ran with it, and he is realizing his future vision. When I ask the second student about the steps he's taken, there's a lot of shrugging and excuses but not much action.

Everything you need to take action and begin slow flipping is on these pages. We've covered the basics of the slow flip formula, how to find and fill slow flips, and the closing process. We've explored not just how private money works, but equally important, the mindset that will draw eager lenders to your program. If you follow and use my approach with potential lenders, you'll operate with confidence and never get rejected. The math on a slow flip is simple, as is the process. With a little hard work and determination, anyone holding this book can become a successful real estate investor using the slow flip method. You don't need money, experience, or exceptional intelligence. You certainly don't need a college degree—I'm living proof of that.

What you do need, more than anything, is to want it. You need to feel that you're destined for something more than the 9–5 grind. You must want to take control of your days, to spend time the way you want to and not the way a boss tells you to. You have to desire freedom. This is why Chapter 1 is actually the most important part of the book. I started with that chapter, on creating your future vision, because it sets the tone for everything and forms the outline of your plan. That plan rests on the foundation of *your* vision and *your* definition of wealth. The italics are there to emphasize that your vision is uniquely yours. It is different for each reader. If four slow flips are all you need to pay the bills and be happy, that's relatively easy. If you need 40 slow flips to feed your taste for luxury cars and European vacations, it's absolutely doable, but it will take a little more time and work. Whatever your "freedom number" is, it should guide everything you do.

The goal here—quick reminder—is freedom, not money or an image. The goal certainly is not to work like a dog for 30 years and then hope that some time remains to enjoy your investment income. Unfortunately, that's the endgame for most of the real estate gurus and big-box seminars promoting the same investment strategies that caused such a debacle around 2008.

As I said, you have everything you need here to start slow flipping, but I realize it's a lot to absorb, especially for readers who are new to real estate. To ease the learning curve, I also offer a free two-hour training that covers the slow flip process, as a companion to this book. At www.SlowFlips.com, readers can register for the next free webinar, which offers a blueprint for slow flipping. It covers information you've already read here, but it can be helpful to have a streamlined overview and a human being talking you through the process, in addition to words on a page. Even if you understand everything you've read in *The Art of the Slow Flip*, I recommend that you invest two hours of your time in this free training to reinforce the core concepts and boost your comfort level.

I'll leave you with one more nudge to get started. If you're nervous about investing in slow flips, don't worry. Everyone is, right out of the gate. The only cure for nervousness is to jump in and start tackling those tasks, performing the steps we've talked about. As you complete them, the anxiety will fade. Of course, you won't do them perfectly at first. We don't need perfect, just adequate, to start. We have a saying, "Done is better than good." While you're spending months on a perfect website and artistic business cards, deals are passing you by. You need to get stuff done, dive into the tasks we've outlined here, and forget about perfection. I often mention a line from an investment seminar I once attended, "If years from now, you look back at the first round of stuff you did and don't laugh about how bad it was, you took too long to get it done."

Those are good words for a slow flipper to live by, though, as I've said, I don't recommend that you buy your first house tomorrow. One of the key steps we talked about involves getting a feel for your local market, or whichever market you want to invest in. My suggestion is that anyone who wants to get into slow flips should look at 100 potential deals and analyze at least 100 properties before buying one. Now, if an amazing opportunity presents itself while you're perusing those first 100, it's fine to make an offer. But when you're starting, it can be difficult to see the difference between a cheap and a deal. After analyzing 100 properties, some will start to stick out. You'll be able to pass by dozens that are merely cheap and stop on the one that has the right combination of condition, quality, and price. You'll develop a knack for spotting the deal, which is critical. The analysis I'm talking about here doesn't take long, and it's well worth your time investment to get a feel for distressed properties in your chosen market and to develop some standards.

You can go online right now and look at the first of those 100 properties to begin educating yourself on your potential market. You can start figuring out what distressed houses in your area look like, sell for, and which submarkets seem most promising. In the next five minutes, you can sign up for free training at www.SlowFlips.com. With a simple online search, you can, right now, look into business cards, signs, a website, a logo, local investor clubs, and polo shirts for your new business ... If you want it, freedom is only five years away. It starts with a few really simple steps. Are you going to take the first of those steps now or push that freedom horizon and your future vision further away? I hope the answer is, "Yes, I'm going to take the first step now."

Do something today that your future self will thank you for.